Welcome!

The Fellowship for Intentional Community is pleased to offer you t[illegible] of our crop—the very best articles that have appeared over the last 20 years in our flagship publications: *Communities* magazine and *Communities Directory*. We've distilled what we consider the most insightful and helpful articles on the topics that you—our readers—have told us you care about most, and have organized them into 15 scintillating collections:

I. Intentional Community Overview; Starting a Community
II. Seeking and Visiting a Community
III. Leadership, Power, and Membership
IV. Good Meetings
V. Consensus
VI. Agreements, Conflict, and Communication
VII. Relationships, Intimacy, Health, and Well-Being
VIII. Children in Community
IX. Community for Elders
X. Sustainable Food, Energy, and Transportation
XI. Green Building, Ecovillage Design, and Land Preservation
XII. Cohousing
XIII. Cooperative Economics and Creating Community Where You Are
XIV. Challenges and Lessons of Community
XV. The Peripatetic Communitarian: The Best of Geoph Kozeny

On average, each collection is comprised of 15–20 articles, containing a total of 55–65 pages. All are available both as downloadable PDFs and as print copies. Buy one, buy several, or buy the whole set! While there's a smattering of classic pieces that date back to the '90s, the vast majority of these offerings have been written in the past dozen years, representing cutting-edge thinking and how-to explorations of the social, ecological, and economic aspects of sustainable living. We've gathered insights about what you can expect when raising children in community, and offer a wealth of information about what it's like to grow old there, too. For dessert, we have the collected wisdom of over 50 essays from Geoph Kozeny (1949–2007), the Peripatetic Communitarian.

If you're hungry for information about cooperative living, we have a menu that will satisfy any appetite! If you're thinking about starting a community, this collection offers an incredible storehouse of practical advice. If you're thinking of joining a community, our packets will help you discern the right things to look for, and how to be a savvy shopper. If you're just curious about community and want to snack, our smörgåsbord of tasty nuggets will let you pick and choose what's most appealing.

Bon appétit!

Laird Schaub
FIC Executive Secretary
November 2013

Intentional Community Overview, and Starting a Community

Many people yearn for community—for a greater sense of connection and belonging—yet genuinely wanting it and accurately knowing that it's good for you are not enough to guarantee that you'll be happy in intentional community, or that others will want to live with you.

These 15 articles provide a peek behind the curtain at some the pitfalls and challenges facing community builders, so that you'll have a more realistic idea of what it will take to survive your start-up years and actually become a home. You'll find first-hand stories from forming communities, as well as sage advice about legal structures, the importance of community spirit, how to understand "cults" as a pejorative label, how to assess prospective property, and the importance of making process agreements *before* you need to apply them.

—Laird Schaub. FIC Executive Secretary, November 2013

In Community, Intentionally

by Geoph Kozeny

"I WANT MORE OF A SENSE OF COMMUNITY in my life." It seems like you hear people saying that all the time these days. What's remarkable is that this inspiration is not coming only from folks that might be called alternative—I hear it from people representing a wide spectrum of values, ideals, and lifestyles.

Not surprisingly, intentional communities also represent a wide spectrum of values and ideas. For thousands of years people have been coming together to share their lives in creative and diverse ways. Today is no different; efforts to create new lifestyles based on shared ideals are as common as ever.

An Intentional Community ...

"is a group of people who have chosen to live or work together in pursuit of a common ideal or vision. Most, though not all, share land or housing. Intentional communities come in all shapes and sizes, and display an amazing diversity in their common values, which may be social, economic, spiritual, political, and/or ecological. Some are rural; some urban. Some live all in a single residence; some in separate households. Some raise children; some don't. Some are secular, some are spiritually based, and others are both. For all their variety though, the communities featured in our magazine hold a common commitment to living cooperatively, to solving problems nonviolently, and to sharing their experience with others."

—*Communities* magazine

Pursuing Dreams

All intentional communities have idealism in common—each one was founded on a vision of living in a better way, usually in response to something perceived as lacking in the broader culture. Many communities aspire to provide a supportive environment for the development of members' awareness, abilities, and spiritual growth. Most seek to create a life that will satisfy shared human cravings: security, family, relationship, fellowship, mutual cooperation, creativity and self-expression, as well as a sense of place, a sense of belonging.

Typically, today's intentional communities are melting pots of ideals and issues that have been in the public spotlight over the decades: equality and civil rights, women's liberation, antiwar efforts, ecology and conservation, alternative energy, sustainable agriculture, co-ops, worker-owned businesses, personal growth, and spirituality. Some groups focus on only one or a few of these areas, while others try to integrate them all into a coherent whole. (You can get a good overview of how broadly groups in this directory focus their vision by using the cross-referencing charts that precede the listings.)

Although intentional communities are usually on the fringes of mainstream culture, the everyday values and priorities of community members are surprisingly compatible with those of their less adventurous counterparts. Both tend to assign value to providing a stable home and good education for their children, finding meaningful and

---

Geoph Kozeny has lived in various kinds of communities for 35 years, and has been on the road for the past 19 years—visiting, studying, facilitating, and consulting for intentional communities all across North America. He asks about their visions and realities, takes photos, and gives multi-media shows about the diversity and vitality of the Communities Movement. He was a core staff member for the first two editions of the *Communities Directory*, and is a regular columnist for *Communities* magazine. In 2002, he released "Visions of Utopia," a full-length video documentary on intentional communities, and is presently editing footage for a second volume. He can be reached via email at *geoph@ic.org*, or write Community Catalyst Project, c/o 1531 Fulton Street, San Francisco, CA 94117, USA.

Susan Patrice

"Communities value providing a stable home and good education for their children, finding meaningful and satisfying work, and living in a safe neighborhood and an unpolluted environment."

satisfying work, living in a safe neighborhood and an unpolluted environment, and participating in local organizations and activities. For many, finding a spiritual path is also important as it can provide a context for the other goals and a basis for making decisions in times of uncertainty. The main difference is that most community members are not satisfied with the status quo. Intentional communities are testing grounds for new ideas about how to maintain more satisfying lives that enable people to actualize more of their untapped potential.

Time Is Not Standing Still

Most communities sound very clear and confident when describing their values, goals, and practices, but such things inevitably evolve over time. When you come across a documentary or a directory listing that profiles a community, I suggest thinking of the description as a snapshot in their family scrapbook. Most of the images—the people, the buildings, the activities, the priorities, even the visions—are subject to change over time.

> After living in six communities over 15 years, I thought I knew what worked best—wrong!

I'm amazed at the number of times I've heard someone say, "I couldn't live in a community without this," or "I could never live in a community that did that"—only to interview them several years later and discover that they were happily living without the former and with the latter. I suspect this lack of wisdom about what we really need and want is due, in part, to the fact that society does not adequately teach us to explore this type of question. Obviously, people's needs change over time as well. On the individual level, needs change as a person matures. On a societal level cultural values and norms shift for many, often inter-related, reasons.

Major changes do occasionally occur overnight in communities. However, it is far more common for large shifts to happen over a more extended period of time. For example, I've visited at least a dozen communities that were radically political in their early years, usually with a population of members mostly in their twenties. Within twenty years, the members—now in their forties—had shifted their focus to improving the quality of their kids' schools, worrying about health concerns, and making plans for their old age.

A Unique Experience

Contrary to popular stereotypes, every branch of the family portrayed in the "scrapbook" is unique. Just as no two brothers, sisters, aunts, uncles, or cousins lead identical lives, no two communities offer precisely the same experience. In the Catholic Worker network, for example, all the houses are based on a core philosophy that was articulated in the 1930s, yet no two are the same. Each community varies according to the number and ages of members, the projects emphasized, local laws and customs, and the cultural backgrounds and personalities of their members.

Likewise, the level of affluence in intentional communities runs the gamut from urban poor, to suburban and rural middle class, to quite well-heeled. Not surprisingly, there is a prevalence of nuclear families, single-parent families, and singles roughly proportionate to what you'd find in the mainstream.

Although there's a full range of ages among the people living in communities—from newborns to those well into their 90s—that diversity does not numerically reflect the demographics of the mainstream. Instead, there is a disproportionate representation of people in the 25- to 50-year-old age range, with the balance skewed toward the older end. Likewise, many cultures and ethnic groups are represented in North American intentional communities, but the well-educated white middle class is represented in proportions greater than in the mainstream.

What Works

After living in six communities over 15 years, I thought I knew what worked best—wrong! Since then I've visited over 300 communities to talk with members and ex-members about their experiences, and to observe what seemed to work and not work. My revised opinion about which structures and decision-making processes work best: whatever the members wholeheartedly believe in.

I've seen reasonably well-functioning examples of communities using consensus, majority voting, inspired anarchy, and benevolent dictatorships. I've also seen examples of each of those styles that seemed dysfunctional and disempowering. Sometimes the same community covered both ends of the spectrum, depending on the issue at hand and what side of the bed community mem-

Flavors of Community

While every community is unique, there are broad ways we can categorize some communities that share important characteristics. Hopefully these definitions can help in our understanding of community, as long as we remember that even within categories communities will vary widely.

Cohousing: Though there is no precise definition, cohousing communities have a variety of typically shared characteristics. Cohousing can appear similar to some mainstream housing developments, but incorporates ideals of participation, cooperation, sharing, and knowing one's neighbors. Most cohousing communities have considerable resident input into the design process as it unfolds, and resident management of the community after it is built. The architectural design generally clusters the housing, with cars de-emphasized and pedestrian/play areas enhanced, to promote frequent and spontaneous human contact. Cohousing communities have a common house, a building/space with a large kitchen and dining room, as well as a range of other facilities desired by the residents. This is intended to act as an extension of the individual private homes, allowing them to be smaller than their non-community counterparts. Most operate by consensus. Work is shared, though work systems vary widely.

Ecovillages: The concept of ecovillage is a vision, an ideal. It combines the principles of ecology (understanding the complex effects of human activities on the environment around us, integration of multiple natural and human systems, sustainability into the indefinite future) and the idea of village (human scaled, with all features needed to meet the basic physical and social needs of its residents). In the real world, an ecovillage is a process toward this general vision. Ecovillages make a commitment to explore various physical and social technologies, and implement those that can move them closer to their vision of this ideal. People from many countries and from many cultures are taking up this challenge. They start from where they are, with widely differing levels of technology and other resources available to them. Each ecovillage asks "How can we use what is available to us to move closer to the ecovillage ideal? What are our strengths that we can share with other ecovillage projects? What do we need that others can help us with?" Each ecovillage finds different answers to these questions, and is at a different point on the path toward its vision.

Kibbutzim: There are 285 kibbutzim (communal settlements) in Israel today. Though most are not religiously focused, a few are. The vast majority are affiliated with the Kibbutz Movement, a pluralistic umbrella organization. While all are more or less politically left wing, kibbutzim have diverged widely from the high level of similarity and centralized economies that characterized the movement just a generation ago. In response to intense economic, political, and generational pressures, most groups have become less communal and allow much more individual choice around finances and job selection. It remains to be seen whether this trend toward diversification and privatization will ultimately produce a stronger, more resilient movement.

bers got out of that day. No amount of theory, dogma, or peer pressure can eliminate the need for clarity of vision, open mindedness, personal integrity, good communication, compassion, the spirit of cooperation, and common sense.

The structure a group uses is merely a tool; how it's applied is what's important. Strong leadership can prove to be inspirational and empowering, or it can prove to be dogmatic and repressive—and the same is true of decentralized individualism. What counts most is a collective sense of well-being, empowerment, and community.

The more egalitarian the group's vision, the more likely that there will be subtle internal power dynamics that go unnoticed, unacknowledged, or are outright denied. This observation is not intended to imply that hierarchies have no inherent problems, including those that produce power struggles, rather that the way they describe their own decision-making process is normally closer to the truth than those groups who aspire to equality. (See Joreen Freeman's article, "The Tyranny of Structurelessness," in the second edition of the *Communities Directory* for a more detailed exploration of this tendency.[1])

While a sense of unity is typically one of the fundamental goals of intentional communities, it is a quality often lacking—sometimes existing only in theory, or deferred as a long-range goal that will be achieved only when the community becomes more "evolved." Unfortunately, we are quite capable of imagining a glorious utopian future without having yet developed many of the skills required to live up to our own high expectations.

Religious/Spiritual Communities: In this category, the variety is quite large. Communities range from long-standing Catholic monasteries and nunneries to the newest New Age groups. Some have a very unified practice, with all in the community sharing a single practice while others have members following a variety of paths. The main thing they all have in common is that they tend to use community as a tool to further their spiritual agenda, rather than as an end in itself. Being gathered into a community allows participants to separate from the temptations and diversions of the outside world, and provides more intense reinforcement for living the focused life of the religious aspirant. We can view spiritual community as a cauldron that creates an intense, focused heat not easily found elsewhere. Many spiritual leaders have recommended or even required that their followers live in a community of believers, as a way to deepen their spiritual life and promote the internal changes that move them closer to the ideal. If you choose to enter the life of a religious community, it is important that you accept the religious practice of the group, without thinking that it will be perfect once you get them to change one or several aspects you don't agree with.

Egalitarian Communities: Some communities explicitly adopt a list of agreements that promote the equality of their members. One group of such communities that is very active in the US Communities Movement is the Federation of Egalitarian Communities (FEC). Each member community agrees to four principal values: egalitarianism, income sharing, cooperation, and non-violence. Each member has equal access to the decision-making process, and to the resources of the community. FEC communities range in size from family size groups to village size, with their decision-making and resource-allocation systems generally becoming more structured and complex as their size increases. Because of the large overlap of shared values, the FEC communities have been able to create and maintain a variety of inter-community connections and projects, including a work exchange program, joint businesses, and a major medical insurance fund.

Student Co-ops: Student housing co-ops are associated with a number of colleges and universities, providing a low-cost alternative to dorms, apartments, fraternities, and sororities. Students often choose co-ops initially for the lower cost, and only discover the interpersonal benefits after they move in. For many young people, student co-ops provide them with their first taste of intentional community. Houses range in size from small houses with a handful of residents, to large buildings that house over a hundred co-opers. Some co-ops restrict members to students while others draw members from the broader community. Student co-ops generally subscribe to the principles of the Co-op Movement, known as the Rochdale principles, written down by a group of weavers in Rochdale, England in 1844. In brief, these are: 1) voluntary and open membership; 2) democratic member control; 3) member economic participation; 4) autonomy and independence; 5) cooperation among cooperatives; and 6) concern for community. The North American Students of Cooperation (NASCO) is the organizational voice of the student Co-op Movement. It provides education, training, networking, and development assistance to existing and new student housing, dining, and business co-ops.

Michael McIntyre – Sunward Cohousing

"Cohousing design generally clusters the housing, with cars de-emphasized and pedestrian/play areas enhanced, to promote frequent and spontaneous human contact."

Novelty and Neighbors

One of the problems with pushing the envelope of mainstream society is running up against laws and regulations that make innovation either illegal, or full of bureaucratic hoops to jump through. Innovative construction styles such as strawbale, cob, and earthships, as well as greywater systems, composting toilets, and organic farming technologies, have until recently been so far outside the norm that local inspectors rarely have a clue about such techniques. As a result, government officials regularly erect hurdles and walls in the path of such alternatives. Fortunately, the innovators have persisted, and local and national codes are slowly embracing alternative technologies.

Zoning regulations, in particular, have proved challenging at times. Numerous cities have laws that prohibit more than three—or in some cases, up to five—unrelated adults from living together in one household. Although such laws were ostensibly instituted to protect neighborhoods from an excess of noise and cars, frequently they are enforced to protect against neighbors displaying nontraditional values and lifestyles. Some of these laws have been overturned in court, but many still exist, and don't usually draw much attention because enforcement is often very lax or nonexistent.

Another set of legal obstacles surfaces around the ownership and financing of commonly held property. Many communities seek to place ownership of their property into a land trust for reasons of affordability, equality, and land stewardship. Land trust philosophy has come a long way over recent decades, but much work has yet to be done before it will be an easily available option in a culture geared toward the sanctity of the individual.

Many community groups are unaware of this history and end up starting the community-building process from scratch.

This is also true with funding. It is rare to find a banker who understands and appreciates cooperation and shared ownership, and that makes financing community-held property difficult. For example, a lack of interim construction financing delayed the start of the Cohousing Movement by several years. It is much easier to secure such funding now that there are nearly five dozen existing prototypes to point to.

Further, because social innovations are often more threatening than technological and economic innovations, relations with neighbors are often hugely challenging. The way neighbors perceive the community—and more importantly, how they interact with it—can run the gamut from generic mistrust and violent hostility to hearty appreciation and mutual cooperation.

When there is a media "cult" scare in the news, some communities—most notably the secretive or isolated groups—experience unfavorable rumors and critical scrutiny from their neighbors. On the other hand, those deeply involved in local activities (thereby having regular face-to-face encounters with folks living nearby) typically experience very little change in their neighborly interactions and the degree of local acceptance.

This variance reflects the tendency in our culture to mistrust strangers and anyone "different from us." Thus when a community settles into a new area, the usual default mode is that the locals will eye the newcomers with suspicion until the newcomers have "proven themselves."

This guilty-until-proven-innocent mentality has been fed by the media since the inception of the tabloid, and probably longer. The prevailing attitude among mainstream publishers is simple: sensational news is what sells newspapers and magazines. Yet, for some reason it seems that most readers fail to take that—and the cultural biases automatically built into so-called objective reporting—into account when assessing what coverage to believe.

As a result, it is the communities that are on familiar and friendly terms with their neighbors that fare the best during times of widespread paranoia. When facts are scarce, the tendency is to fill the gaps with imagination. Unfortunately, these projections do not often give newcomers the benefit of the doubt.

Reinventing Wheels

Most of these "unique new ideas" are neither new, nor unique. They seem so to us only because they're not commonly discussed or covered in standard history texts or daily news. People throughout the world have been trying out similar—if not identical—ideas over many centuries, often bucking resistance and persecution.

Many community groups are unaware of this history and end up starting the community-building process from scratch. There is also a tendency to resist advice from outside experts, usually because of a mistrust of outsiders, or a diehard sense that "We need to be able to do this for ourselves if our model is to be self-sufficient and sustainable." The reality is that the insights of an outsider—someone experienced with the issues at hand, but not caught up in the internal dynamics of the community—can often provide the exact piece of information or insight needed to break through an impasse and move the community toward a constructive resolution.

One way around this tendency toward isolation is to develop sister communities and networks built around common ideals and interests—the raison d'être for the FIC and this directory. Communities in close association with one another can share ideas, resources, and mutual support, thereby benefiting from each other's assets and experience. In addition, community networks can create common funds to do outreach, develop community-based business ventures, and cover medical emergencies (in lieu of expensive insurance policies that drain working capital out of the movement).

Communities in close association with one another can share ideas, resources, and mutual support, thereby benefiting from each other's assets and experience.

It Ain't Easy

Over the centuries well-intentioned attempts to live in community have generated a huge list of casualties. Countless thousands of folks have been inspired by a vision of a better world, and eventually ended up completely frustrated by the discrepancy between the vision and the reality.

At first glance this might seem peculiar, but it's exactly what should be expected, as most of us are products of an imperfect, overly competitive, alienating society. Although we tend to be aware of some of our negative conditioning, most of it is beyond the grasp of our limited worldview. If we're serious about creating a better world, we need to start with ourselves.

If you should happen to hear a glowing report about the perfect community somewhere, one with no rough edges, presume you're not getting the whole story. There's probably a shadow side somewhere that's unexplored and needs to be acknowledged before the members will be able to work through, rather than avoid, the underlying issues.

Conflict is inevitable, and traditionally it is handled so poorly that many of us have learned to dread it and avoid it. However, conflict is a useful indicator of points of non-alignment. Working creatively with these points usually results in tremendous positive growth spurts for everyone involved, both individually and collectively. The key to using conflict constructively is to get the affected parties to believe that a solution is possible, and to commit their best effort to finding a solution that works for all.

Every one of us brings along our own baggage wherever we go, and a supportive cooperative environment is the best possible place for us to explore our personal growing edge. It will prove to be the most challenging and frustrating inner work we've ever attempted, but if we pick the right people to work with, and approach it with the right attitude, it's entirely worth it—the best path available for actualizing our full potential.

Endnotes

1. Joreen Freeman's article from the second edition of the *Communities Directory*, "The Tyranny of Structurelessness," is also available on the Web, at http://www.ic.org/pnp/cdir/1995/23joreen.html

Setting the Record Straight:

13 myths about intentional community

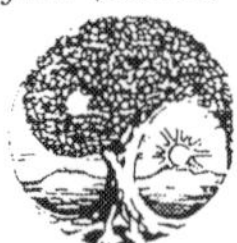

FELLOWSHIP NEWS

by Diana Leafe Christian, Geoph Kozeny, Laird Schaub

One of the tasks of the Fellowship for Intentional Community is helping the public understand that the communities movement exists, is growing, and is a good thing. That often requires debunking common myths and misconceptions. Here's a list that the FIC hands out to journalists—to set the record straight.

Myth: There are no intentional communities anymore; they died out in the '60s & '70s.
Fact: Not so. Many of those communities survived and thrived, and many new ones have formed since. A significant surge of new interest in intentional communities began in the '90s. The FIC has about 3,000 North American communities in its database, and estimates that there are thousands more.

Myth: Intentional communities are all alike.
Fact: There is enormous diversity among intentional communities. While most communities share land or housing, and members share a common vision and work actively to carry out their common purpose, the vision can vary widely from community to community. Some communities have been formed to share resources, create great family neighborhoods, or live ecologically sustainable lifestyles. Some are wholly secular, others are committed to a common spiritual practice; many are spiritually eclectic. Some help war refugees, the urban homeless, or developmentally disabled children. Some operate rural conference and retreat centers, health and healing centers, or sustainable-living education centers.

Myth: Intentional communities are all "communes."
Fact: Many people use these terms interchangeably. It is probably more useful to use the term "commune" as an economic term, for communities operating with a common treasury and sharing ownership of their property. Few intentional communities are actual communes.

Myth: Most community members are young—in their twenties.
Fact: Most communities are multi-generational.

Myth: Most communitarians are hippies.
Fact: Few communities today identify with the hippie stereotype, and many are cohousers, who essentially live a middle-class, though more cooperative, lifestyle. Most communitarians tend to be politically left of center, hard-working, peace-loving, health-conscious, environmentally concerned, and family-oriented.

Myth: All intentional communities are out in the boondocks.
Fact: About half of the communities listed in the 2000 Communities Directory

are rural, about a fourth are urban, some have both rural and urban sites, and some don't specify.

Myth: Most intentional communities are organized around a particular religion or common spiritual practice.
Fact: While it's true that many groups have a spiritual focus—statistics from the 2000 Communities Directory show that half are secular, 10 percent don't specify, and 40 percent have a spiritual focus. Of these, some are religious, some have a common spiritual practice, and some are spiritually eclectic.

Myth: Most intentional communities have an authoritarian form of governance; they follow a charismatic leader.
Fact: The reverse is true; the most common form of governance is democratic, with decisions made by some form of consensus or voting. Of the hundreds of communities listed in the 1995 Directory, for example, 64 percent were democratic, nine percent had a hierarchical or authoritarian structure, 11 percent were a combination of democratic and hierarchical. Many communities which formerly followed one leader or a small group of leaders have changed in recent years to a more democratic form of governance.

Myth: Community members all think alike.
Fact: Because communities are, by definition, organized around a common vision or purpose, their members tend to hold a lot of values and beliefs in common—many more than are shared among a typical group of neighbors. Still, disagreements are a common occurrence in most communities, just as in the wider society.

Myth: Most communities are "cults."
Fact: Both the American Psychological Association and the Society for the Scientific Study of Religion have done research that refutes the idea that religious or other groups are systematically brainwashing their members or interfering with their ability to think critically.

Although the term "cult" is usually intended to identify a group in which abuse occurs, it would generally be a more accurate description if the observer defined a cult as "a group with values and customs different from mine; a group that makes me feel uncomfortable or afraid."

Most communities are not abusive toward members. The ones that are, especially those prone to violence, can attract media attention which falsely implies that intentional communities are abusive in general. It's our experience that the overwhelming majority of communities are considered good places to live by their members—and good neighbors by people who live around them.

Myth: Community members have little privacy or autonomy.
Fact: The degree of privacy and autonomy in communities varies as widely as the kinds of communities themselves. In some communities individual households own their own land and house, and have their own independent economy (perhaps with shared facilities); their degree of privacy and autonomy is nearly identical to that of mainstream society. In most cohousing communities, for example, residents enjoy autonomy similar to that of any planned housing development. However, in communities with specific religious or spiritual lifestyles (such as monasteries or some meditation retreats), privacy and autonomy are typically more limited, as part of the purpose for which the community was organized. Most communities fall between these two points on the privacy/held-in-common spectrum. Many older communities have become more privatized and less communal over the years.

Myth: Most members of intentional communities live impoverished lifestyles with limited resources.
Fact: Communities make a wide variety of choices regarding standard of living—some embrace voluntary simplicity, while others emphasize full access to the products and services of today's society. Nearly all communities take advantage of sharing and the opportunities of common ownership to allow individuals access to facilities and equipment they don't need to own privately (for example, power tools, washing machines, pickup trucks, and, in some cases, even

swimming pools).

Members of new communities that start off with limited resources tend to live simply. As they mature, they tend to create a stable economic base and enjoy a more comfortable life—according to their own standards. Many established communities have built impressive facilities, financed by successful community businesses, such as light manufacturing, food products, computer services, and conference centers.

Myth: Most people who live in communities are running away from responsibilities.
Fact: Many people choose to live in community because it offers an alternative way of life from that of the wider society, yet most community members still raise families, maintain and repair their land and buildings, work for a living, pay taxes, etc.

At the same time, communitarians usually perceive their lifestyle as more caring and satisfying than that of mainstream culture, and because of this—and the increased free time which results from pooling resources and specialized skills—many community members feel they can engage more effectively with the wider society. Ω

Diana Leafe Christian is editor of Communities magazine. Laird Schaub is the Executive Secretary of the Fellowship for Intentional Community. Geoph Kozeny, the magazine's "Peripatetic Communitarian" columnist, is producer/editor of a three-hour video documentary about communities.

A COMMUNITARIAN CONUNDRUM: Why a World That Wants and Needs Community Doesn't Get It

By Timothy Miller

The following is an edited version of a paper presented at the annual meeting of the Communal Studies Association, New Harmony, Indiana, October 2, 2010.

I believe that people the world over long for community. While that assertion is just about impossible to test, a number of indicators point in that direction. Social alienation seems to me widespread, with large numbers of people dissatisfied with the prevailing way the world is organized. They may have radically different visions of an ideal world, but a fair number, it is reasonable to guess, see lack of community as a cause of much of the restlessness and anomie we see all around us. The kinds of community that can bring meaning into life are many, but it is another fair guess that more than a few of those longing for community see intentional community as something that could put meaning and fulfillment into their lives.

Communal Aspirations

One bit of evidence for the desire for community can be seen in the classified advertising section, called "Reach," in COMMUNITIES magazine. In every issue there are ads seeking members for established communities, but also quite a few ads for new communities, typically ones that have not yet been actually launched, but concrete visions of community, at least, in the minds of would-be founders and members. In the Fall 2010 issue of the magazine, for example, people were invited to help start an ecovillage and retreat center in Kansas, a desert community in Arizona, a cohousing community in California, an urban cooperative in Hawai'i, and a shared household in New Jersey.

Another bit of evidence for community-mindedness is the traffic on the Fellowship for Intentional Community website. As of October 2010, that site attracted about 66,500 hits per month, or about 2,200 a day, with 6.5 page views per visit, and the numbers for 2010 were up 11 percent over 2009. While not everyone visiting the site is in the market for community, surely the numbers reflect to some degree interest in intentional communities—if not living in one, at least wishing.

Video sales also indicate increased interest in community. The FIC reports that it sold over 1000 total copies of the two volumes of Geoph Kozeny's video "Visions of Utopia" last year, and that included more sales of volume 1 than had been reached in any of the seven years it has been available.

Communities also attract attention from the broader public. There is a steady stream of media coverage of communities, as in the case of a photo feature on East Wind community in *National Geographic* in 2005. And there is a steady stream of visitors to communities—not just sightseers, but in many cases persons looking for a place to live in community.

The Hard Numbers

For all of the interest there seems to be in intentional communities, however, the number of persons actually living in intentional communities is tiny—a very small fraction of 1 percent of the population. Counting the number of active com-

Labyrinth at New Harmony.

Amana church.

Photos courtesy of Timothy Miller

munitarians is a daunting task, to say the least, but the numbers are not large.

I decided I would count up the population of the hundreds of American communities in the 2007 edition of the *Communities Directory* (the new 2010 directory was not yet out when I did my counting, but I don't think the results there would be very different) and in round numbers that would come to something like 10,000 adults living in communities of five or more members each in the United States. But there are so many problems with the numbers that getting within even a couple of orders of magnitude is dubious. For example, the Adidam community lists its population at 1060. But that apparently includes many locations, the majority of them outside the United States. On the other hand, the Bruderhof communities don't provide any numbers at all, and that group of communities, with a membership thought to be in the low thousands, has enough members that its numbers alone would have quite an impact on any total figure. And the most important skewing factor of all is that huge numbers of communities choose not to be listed in the directory.

So I took another path toward trying to make an estimate. The Catholic religious communities keep pretty careful track of their numbers; in 2007 they reported 13,428 priests, 60,715 sisters, and 4,904 brothers, for a total communal population of 79,048.[1] There are two other groups of communities with five-figure populations, the Mormon fundamentalists, who are thought to have perhaps 30,000 communal members, and the Hutterites, who have around 15,000 in the United States. So that puts us at around 125,000 communitarians. Now, here is the wildest guess of all: I'm going to conjecture that there are 5,000 other intentional communities averaging 10 members apiece, which would be another 50,000. Add that to the 125,000 we already have, and, just to be cautious, let's report the total as a range: 150,000 to 200,000.

The point of all this guesswork is to say that not a lot of people live communally. Given an American population of over 300 million, 150,000 is fewer than 1 in 2,000, less than 1/20 of 1 percent of the population; 200,000 is fewer than 1 in 1,500, less than 1/15 of 1 percent of the population. And take out the Catholic communities, which are linked to a larger tradition that provides a support system, and focus only on independent, freestanding communities, and the numbers are even more drastic. We probably have fewer than 100,000 such communitarians, which comes to fewer than 1 in 3,000 Americans, less than 1/30 of 1 percent of the population. No matter how you slice it, communal living is not a mass movement.

So why not, if so many people long for community in their lives?

Some Reasons for the Gap

One answer is that community in the broad sense doesn't necessarily involve a residential situation that meets even a simple definition of intentional community. So the communitarian desires of many can be met through various non-residential forms of close relationships—churches, social organizations, political organizations, fraternal organizations, and many other such institutions. But the gap remains. Why do so few people live in community?

Many who have considered the disconnect between a widespread desire for community and the difficulty of starting actual communities and getting them to function well have focused on what might be called internal issues—things such as interpersonal relations, decision-making processes, leadership, and financial strength. Many accounts of communal life, especially of short-lived communities, talk about internal bickering, conflicts between leaders and the rank and file, and inadequate work skills on the part of members, especially when a community is trying to make a living through agriculture. Take just about any issue of COMMUNITIES magazine over the last several years and you will find those things—especially personal relations and group process—discussed at length.

However, issues that could be called external may be more important than the internal ones. American society, in particular, has structures and attitudes that discourage communal ventures. I would like to look at some of the ways in which our contemporary American lifestyle impedes the development of communal living.

One fundamental problem is what I will call, for lack of a better term, basic American selfishness. Our whole national ethos seems to be predicated on a me-first approach to life, something that is about as contrary to communitarianism as anything could be. Little acts of me-first rudeness are all around us, as in the case of my neighbors who needlessly park half blocking the alley and make it hard for the rest of us to get through, whose free-range cats methodically kill the songbirds we try to attract, and whose dog is left outside to bark all night.

The "Reach" pages of COMMUNITIES magazine bring this all-American tendency into focus quite clearly: while in every issue several communities advertise that they are looking for new members, just as many ads ask for new members to join a community founder's new or prospective venture. One way to interpret this: I don't want to work within someone else's vision; I want people to help me work out my own plan. That kind of attitude, if it's there, really negates any possibility of community, since the diminution of the will and the ego are essential to any communal venture. American individualism is deeply ingrained in us, and I think that is one fundamental reason why most people don't join communities, despite their manifold attractions.

Another basic problem, one that could be solved legislatively but may never be, is zoning. Zoning laws have existed in this country for less than a century, so when the Shakers and Harmonists and Amana colonists set up shop, for example, zoning was one problem they didn't have to worry about. When they bought land, they could use it as they liked. If they mixed commercial and industrial and residential uses in some unconventional way, no problem. But since the early 20th century zoning has been implemented in much of the country.

The desire for zoning is certainly understandable; I don't want my neighbor to sell her house to make way for a 24-hour fast-food restaurant with a drive-up window and bright lights and lots of litter. However, perhaps inadvertently, zoning laws have seriously impeded intentional communities. In many parts of my city if more than three people occupy a house, they must all be related. That means that my lesbian

Shaker barn, Hancock Shaker Village.

neighbors, a couple with children who are forbidden by law to marry and who are the best neighbors you could ever want, could be run out of their home if a moral crusader were to go after them. If such innocuous people are threatened by zoning laws, how much more are communitarians unable to pursue their dreams? I know of a large intentional community that has around 60 resident members and tries to keep an utterly low profile in order to avoid attracting attention to itself. The community is located in a county where officials have bulldozed two intentional communities they deemed illegal, so the remaining community's fears are not exactly unfounded. How unfair is that?

Technology vs. Community

Another broad category of modern anti-communitarian forces at work in our society consists of technological devices, including many that we almost all use. Perhaps the biggest offender here is the automobile, which, despite its enormous convenience, seems to bring out the worst in many people who use it. Where I live people are fairly courteous with each other face to face; we open doors for others, we say please and thank you, we wait our turn in line rather than cutting in.

Yet large numbers act aggressively and rudely and irresponsibly all too often when they are behind the wheel of a car, running red lights and cutting people off and speeding at just about all times. Although someone who did a controlled study of motoring behavior might come up with some other answer, my own conclusion is that the automobile is an inherently isolating device, one that enables relative anonymity, and that it seems to give the anonymous driver a chance to behave in an unfriendly way without really being seen. I've wondered, sometimes, if we would have more courteous driving if the name of each principal driver were painted onto the car in large graphics.

A street corner in New Harmony.

If the automobile is anti-communal, so is television, and as television technology progresses, it seems to draw ever more people away from social interaction. Entertainment was once largely communal; people would mingle with others at dances, concerts, movies, and other such events held in public spaces. Television, which the average American watches for several hours a day, draws people away from such activities and reinforces the value of being alone.

Even worse than television, at least potentially, is the near-universal spread of the cell phone. People once walked down the street looking at the people around them, looking at the surrounding environment, and occasionally greeting those they encountered, but today hordes of people walk everywhere with cell phones held firmly to the sides of their heads. That primary focus on cell conversation tends to lead them to avoid eye contact and to withdraw from other interaction. We know, of course, how vital the typical cell phone conversation is. On campus the ones I overhear usually go something like this: "Oh, not much. What're you doing? Maybe I'll go find something to eat. Want to talk later? Give me a call." I have instructed my students not to use their cell phones in class, but then I go to faculty gatherings and watch people there texting rather than paying attention to the work at hand, or jumping up and running out of the room to take calls at will. Many of us worry about the danger of cell phone use by drivers; research has shown that using a cell phone creates a distraction that is on average the equivalent of a blood-alcohol level of 0.12 percent, or one and a half times the legal limit for alcohol in most states. Texting, of course, is much worse than that.

Center family dwelling, Pleasant Hill Shaker Village.

But I digress. Bad driving is hardly the only product of cell-phone use; decline of human community is just as serious. Incidentally, one byproduct of cell phones is also unfortunate: we are experiencing a serious decline and soon, probably, the extinction of phone books, with which we can locate each other easily—another anticommunal effect, in other words.

Computers have brought a lot of convenience into our lives, but they too can be seriously anticommunal. Initially the computer was a great means of social contact for far-flung intentional communities, but its net effect has moved strongly over to the dark side. Probably the biggest culprit is social networking, which, although it does promote personal interaction, puts people in front of monitors or on their cell phones rather than in personal contact with others. Once again prospects for human interaction are hindered when they should be helped.

Even air conditioning takes its toll on community. When the weather is hot, most of us like to stay inside where it's cool. That's not a very good way to interact with one's neighbors, and it certainly has nothing but negative environmental impacts.

Alternatives to all of these isolating technologies exist. We can do much of our moving about with public transit and walking; we can find entertainment live instead of on television; we can, at least for the moment, still find public telephones in public places if we do need to communicate while away from home or office, and therefore not really need a cell phone. Front porches and public swimming pools can help minimize the need for air conditioning. We can gather, at least occasionally, face-to-face instead of on Facebook. But that's not the way things are headed in these last declining days of Western civilization.

The "C" Words

Now, I don't want to end by saying that technology is the sole culprit in the decline of American communal values, or the sole impediment to the growth of intentional communities. There is one other social presence that might be even worse than isolating technology, and that is a suspicion of cooperation that is both wide and deep.

That suspicion would seem to be a product of modern history. Charles Nordhoff, writing in 1875, could call his book *The Communistic Societies of the United States* without undue controversy, and others in the communities movement of the 19th century used the word in a positive and uncontroversial way. The 20th century, however, was the era of evil communism, or Marxism. Until the fall of the Soviet Union and its related states 20 years ago there was no more horrifying word in the English language than "communism," and although today its definitive horrifics have been replaced by terms such as Al Qaida and terrorism, its demonizing power remains strong. Socialism too remains a term of enormous opprobrium, as we have seen when universal health care is labeled socialist and therefore condemned.

The effect of anticommunist and antisocialist fervor on intentional communities is not just hypothetical. In the 1930s communitarians were acutely aware of the persecution they faced when their way of life became known, and tended to keep their profiles low. In the 1940s the New Deal communities of the Resettlement Administration and other agencies, which helped thousands of families up from abject poverty through cooperative rural projects, were summarily shut down by Congress precisely because of their collective nature. A few years earlier public officials in the state of Arkansas became determined to purge the nest of radicals at the communal Commonwealth College—note that name, *Commonwealth*—from their midst, and in 1940 state action did effectively put the college out of business.

Confronting the Challenges

All of these things add up to a powerful anticommunitarian bias in American life. Intentional communities, especially in their modern forms as ecovillages and cohousing, have a great deal to offer a world with pressing social and environmental problems. But the forces running in the other direction are formidable, and if the communities movement is to rise to its full potential, those forces must be identified and dealt with. That is a project of enormous dimensions. ❧

Timothy Miller, professor of religious studies at the University of Kansas, presented a version of this paper at the annual meeting of the Communal Studies Association, New Harmony, Indiana, October 2, 2010.

AMY SOPHIA MARASHINSKY

You Know You Live in Community When . . .

BY VIRGINIA LORE AND MARIL CRABTREE

- You don't have to go to a bookstore to find a good read.
- You can't remember the last time you took the trash out.
- You can always find someone to take you to the airport, watch your pets, water your plants, and eat your brownies.
- Someone's always up for a hike or a hot tub.

- You've talked about world peace, the global economy, and the Bush administration—all before breakfast.
- You know at least one person who has been arrested for demonstrating their beliefs.
- You know what "polyamory" means.

- You feel guilty about your TV viewing habits—if you have any.
- You have to try 14 keys to find the one you want.

- You know a dozen ways to cook tofu.

- Your parenting style regularly comes up for review.
- Your spending habits regularly come up for review.

- There's always something fattening in the kitchen.
- The leftovers are still there only because you hid them in a yogurt tub.
- Laundry day is any day the washer is free.

- You've had to sell your kayak because the community already has two.
- The question "but where will we put it?" plays a big role in your buying decisions.

- Honoring the process is more important than making the decision.

- Deciding when to start planting the community garden requires the negotiation skills of Bishop Tutu.
- You know someone who has carried a grudge since 1972 when the mailboxes were reorganized without consensus.
- You hate to admit it, but you're that person.

- You fantasize more about winning a weekend getaway than about winning the lottery.
- Other people's kids call you "Mommy."
- You know where to go for a hug.

Virginia Lore is a cofounder of Duwamish Cohousing in Seattle, Washington; Maril Crabtree is a cofounder of Hearthaven, an urban community in Kansas City, Missouri. Both have contributed previously to Communities magazine. Virginia is Maril's daughter.

"Cults" and Intentional Communities

Working Through Some Complicated Issues

by Tim Miller

A FAIR NUMBER OF PEOPLE BELIEVE our society is swarming with dangerous cults, religious (and sometimes political or social) organizations that are terribly destructive to their members and a real danger to society at large. For better or worse, intentional communities are often drawn into the "cult" controversy. Communities, after all, in many cases do have features that many consider cultic. Individual will sometimes takes the back seat for the good of the group. Some communities have strong-minded leaders. Commitment to the group can run high. Because of these similarities, communitarians cannot altogether escape the great American cult controversy.

While off-course groups and dysfunctional—or even outright evil—individuals may exist, my own conclusion is that, by and large, the cult scare is seriously overblown. To say the least, many of the most frequent allegations about cult activities don't hold up under scrutiny. Groups that represent a real threat to the public do not number many thousands, nor do their members number hundreds of thousands, or even millions, as some anti-cult activists assert. Unless, of course, one preposterously considers every Hindu temple, Muslim mosque, and intentional community a dangerous "cult."

Equally erroneous is the assertion that the cult menace is growing. Religions with unconventional appeal have been around as long as civilization, and the fear of the different is just as ancient as those alternative pathways. While not all traditions, groups, and persons are wholesome, most are relatively innocuous. One wishes that the generalized anti-cult denunciations that are so easy to throw around were based on real case-by-case evidence, not the sort of spectral hysteria that fueled the Salem witch trials.

If I could choose just one step forward in the cult controversy, it would consist of the abandonment of the term "cult" itself. As Catherine Wessinger once wrote in *Communities* magazine, "The word 'cult,' which formerly referred to an organized system of worship, is now a term that slanders any religion that you don't know about and don't like." And that does matter; when a society tolerates pejorative language, it announces that some people are marginal, even subhuman.

Hateful thought, we have painfully learned, can lead to hateful acts. The widespread belief that destructive cults are proliferating and posing a grave danger to society has led to atrocities. Many who have studied the Waco siege and fire believe that the federal agents at the scene badly overestimated the danger that the Branch Davidians posed to society. There was very little understanding about just who the Davidians were and what they believed, which contributed to a situation in which several dozens of innocent people—many of them children—were killed.

People who see these shadowy groups as a major social menace often draw up lists of generalizations by which a savvy observer should be able to identify out-of-control groups. The problem is that the items on those lists almost always apply just as fully to good, healthy groups as to problematic ones. Consider these items from the typical cult-hazard list:

"A cult has a strong, powerful, dominant leader." But

Tim Miller teaches in the Department of Religious Studies at the University of Kansas, where he specializes in alternative religions and intentional communities. He is the editor of *America's Alternative Religions* and author of *The Quest for Utopia in Twentieth-Century America* and *The 60s Communes*. He may be reached at the Department of Religious Studies, University of Kansas, 1300 Oread St, Lawrence KS 66045, USA. Email: *tim@ic.org*.

that doesn't identify inherently dangerous situations. Alan Greenspan, the head of the Federal Reserve System, is enormously powerful and makes decisions that deeply affect the lives of all of us, so is he automatically a cult leader?

"A cult works extremely zealously to attract new members." But missionary zeal is a crucial element of Christianity, Islam, and other religions the world over. Most religions are always very happy to receive new members. You can believe that you know the ultimate truth and work hard to get others to accept your version of truth without deserving to be considered a social menace.

"A cult is preoccupied with getting money." A lot of groups sure do want your money—from religious groups to an array of nonprofits, and back again. While it is sad that our social institutions seem so uniformly thirsty for cash, it clearly shows the situation is not unique to cults.

"Cults suppress questioning and doubt." Many religious sects believe that they embody the truth, and urge followers to promulgate that truth, rather than seriously debate it.

"Indoctrination techniques help keep people involved in the group." Most groups have rituals and practices that push members to stay involved. It's possible (at a stretch) to see things like meditation, chanting, speaking in tongues, and group yoga as manipulative, but they don't cause otherwise sane people to lose their free will.

"A cult imposes major lifestyle restrictions on members, sometimes telling them what clothes to wear, how to raise their children, and even whom to marry." Most groups are not all that restrictive, but a few, indeed, are. Hardly any, however, are more restrictive than a Catholic religious community that tells its members they can't marry, can't have much money, and must follow a strict code of conduct. Most people wouldn't choose that, but those who voluntarily choose a restricted, guided lifestyle often find it empowering. Ask any nun about that.

"Cult members often cut off ties with their birth families and old friends in favor of total dedication to the cult." Actually, that's just what Jesus advised his followers to do; see Matthew 19:29 and Luke 14:26.

"Cult members are asked to give huge amounts of their time to the group." All religions and most social groups urge their members to be highly dedicated to group purposes. Hard workers are prized. And what's so bad about working hard for a cause in which one believes? Building community isn't easy, and the most dedicated are the ones who make it happen.

All of that is not to say that abuses don't occur, that people don't get hurt. People do get exploited, and well-intentioned people get taken advantage of in every corner of our society—in child care, in schools, in religious organizations, in offices and businesses, in intentional communities, and everywhere else. What's unfair is singling out small religious organizations and intentional communities for special persecution just because they happen to fit someone's preconceptions about cults. People have the right to basic freedoms as long as they're not hurting others, and they should be regarded as innocent until proven guilty. When truly abusive situations do occur, call the police. Short of that, friendly dialogue is usually possible if one retains an open mind.

The average person encounters thousands of individuals, groups, and communities in a lifetime, and inescapably has to work through a never-ending process of making judgments about them. If you encounter an intentional community or a religious group you need to evaluate, I would suggest keeping precepts like these in mind:

Different is not always pathological, and normal is not always safe.

- Different is not always pathological, and normal is not always safe. Some groups can be wildly unconventional yet utterly harmless; others can look very normal, superficially, and still be deeply flawed.
- People have different needs. One person's great communitarian or religious experience can be another's worst nightmare.
- Double standards are unfair. Small, offbeat groups should have the same rights and privileges as large, well-established ones. Lots of groups of all sizes and types are eagerly looking for new members, for example, and it is not any more wrong for a small, unconventional community to urge you to join than it is for the biggest church or social club in town to do so.
- One should take responsibility for one's own actions. One of the most frequent allegations against cults is that they engage in brainwashing of prospective members. Actually, there is no definitive scientific evidence that brainwashing really exists. Most people under most circumstances are capable of making decisions that are right for them and usually have mainly themselves to blame when they make unwise ones.
- The nature of personal relations is subtle and never the same twice. One individual may encounter a given group and find it the best thing that ever happened to him or her; another person may find the same group disgusting. People need to find their own congenial relationships. Joining a group is rather like romance—the chemistry that makes it magical is different in every case.

Behaviors often criticized as signs of abusive situations do not necessarily identify a dysfunctional religious group or community. What, then, should a prospective communitarian do to avoid falling in with a bad crowd?

The basic answer is eternal vigilance. One should be on the lookout all the time—and probably more so in regular, daily life than in a communal situation. Keep both eyes open, and don't let emotion get in the way of common sense. Be wary of persons who are both authoritarian and convinced that they have all the answers. Most communities are wonderful, uplifting places that provide their members with good, meaningful lives, but a few fall short of the mark. If you'll indulge me in one last list, here are a few final tips on staying centered in life:

- Trust your instincts. If you don't feel good about a person or situation, remain skeptical until your doubts have been resolved.
- Don't give your money away unless you are willing to let it go unconditionally and never see it again.
- Remember that things are not always what they initially seem; keep your options open even as you begin to take steps toward serious commitment.
- Question authority.
- Stay away from people who have guns.
- Remember that life goes on; if you make a mistake, extract yourself from it and get on with things.

Communities, on the whole, are the greatest! With a bit of prudent common sense, living in the company of others can be the best experience life has to offer.

Resources/Notes

Many calm and reflective books on nonmainstream religions provide a useful counterpoint to the rather sensational array of popular volumes that have contributed so heavily to the widespread public fear of the influence and growth of cults.

All of the works of the British sociologist of religion Eileen Barker offer useful insights; perhaps the most direct is *New Religious Movements: A Practical Introduction* (Unipub, London, 1989).

John A. Saliba, a Jesuit priest, knows a lot about disciplined community living; his books, especially *Understanding New Religious Movements* (Grand Rapids, Michigan, 1995), are fair, measured, and quietly rational.

Mariana Caplan, who lives in the Hohm Community in Arizona, offers solid personal insights into the stresses that occur in families when children make religious or personal choices not pleasing to their parents in her book *When Sons and Daughters Choose Alternative Lifestyles* (Hohm Press, Prescott, Arizona, 1996), and offers practical suggestions for getting beyond hostility and stereotyping in the generational conflict.

A website that seeks to provide dispassionate inofrmation about a wide array of groups is the *Religious Movements* homepage, *www.religiousmovements.org*. In the interest of full disclosure, I am one of the editors of that website.

My own perspectives on cult issues are elaborated at greater length in a theme section on "Intentional Communities and 'Cults'" that I edited for *Communities* magazine, No. 88, Fall 1995.

Susan Patrice

"With a bit of prudent common sense, living in the company of others can be the best experience life has to offer."

ADAM GRANDIN

"The word 'community' can conjure up images of a place where everyone looks after each other, where everyone feels at home." Sandhill Farm's 25th Anniversary celebration.

COMMUNITY SPIRIT, COMMUNITY 'GLUE'

BY GEOPH KOZENY

Over the past decade, the word "community" has enjoyed a major resurgence in popularity, and has become a buzzword used to conjure up images of togetherness, cooperation, well-being, and a sense of belonging. The primal feeling evoked is that a community is a safe haven—a place where everyone looks after each other, where everyone feels at home, where everyone's needs are met.

SO BEGINS A CLIP FROM THE OPENING DIALOGUE OF "Visions of Utopia," my two-hour video documentary about intentional communities, in the hopper for three years now (due for release this summer!). One of my primary objectives was to capture, for each of the 18 featured communities, a sense of the "glue" that holds them together.

From what I've seen, it appears that the most important ingredient in this brew is how the members of a particular community *feel* about their situation, rather than anything that is truly objective and measurable. To be sure, it's important to have shared goals and shared practices, but in terms of experiencing "community glue," it's the connections, more than the accomplishments, that make the difference.

I looked over the list of 18 communities and made a matrix to assess what their "values glue" might be. It was an interesting exercise, in part because it was so subjective. I realized that my ratings were very intuitive, and would differ somewhat each time I filled out the grid. Further, the ratings were based on my sense of each community—which might not match the communities' own self-evaluations—and I would typically get varying answers if I looked at a group's founding vision as compared to its current reality, or at its written vision statement versus the feel of the community in its everyday life. What I ended up asking myself was, "How much energy, how many resources, and how much emphasis does each community put into this area today?" *(Please see sidebar, "Values of the Featured Communities.")*

My analysis suggests that the top five values shared by these communities are cooperation, a sense of neighborhood and/or community, equality/democracy, shared resources, and a safe environment.

In assessing how well each of the communities has been doing in terms of living up to their stated goals, I give the overall group a high rating. Not that any one of them has become a "Utopia" materialized—yet each community is a pretty fine place to live, and I've been quite impressed by the vision, dedication, and openness of the folks I've interviewed for the video. However, as noted in the matrix, the magic comes not so much from the focus, be it ever so lofty and worthwhile, but from the community members' sense of connection.

I don't mean to imply that accomplishments are not important, because, in fact, working together on a shared project is one of the major ways that we humans manage to get a taste of community. However, several other factors increase the probability that an individual will actually experience a sustained sense of "community spirit" in his or her life. In his or her community, for example:

It's the connections, more than the accomplishments, that make the difference.

• Do community members spend much time together—working, eating, worshipping, socializing, and so on?

• Are people generally supportive and helpful—do they pitch in when an extra hand is needed?

• Is there much time and opportunity for casual interactions—popping in at the neighbor's to borrow a cup of sugar, or stopping to chat in the commons, or just "hanging out"?

• Are the members good at integrating folks on the fringes, and able to bring together people of differing backgrounds, interests, ages, needs?

• How well do the members really know each other—core values, likes and dislikes, idiosyncrasies, childhood issues, prejudices, insecurities?

• How open are they to talking about things that are meaningful to them?

• How good are they at bringing up frustrations, criticisms, and so on—and how effective is the group at working through the issues and the feelings that come up?

CAROL SIMONS

Do community members generally pitch in when help is needed? Digging the latrine at Common Place Land Trust, New York.

• How creative are they, collectively or individually, at helping individuals assess their stuck places and finding ways to manifest positive growth and change?

• Do community members have ways of acknowledging whatever growth and change actually does happen, for example celebrating individual and group accomplishments, of honoring births, deaths, assorted other losses, and rites of passage?

A group of people certainly doesn't need to have all of these social skills to enjoy a deeply connected sense of community, though the more these skills are manifest, the more likely an individual member will feel connected. It helps to cultivate connections in every way possible. Community longevity can also help. The longer folks live under the same roof, or sit at the same table, or work on the same committee, the more likely it is they will experience that intangible sense of being somehow linked in community. In that context, patience and perseverance are great assets.

In contrast, at some of the larger communities, and even at one of the small ones, I noticed some members who had more or less withdrawn from the daily life of the community, and whose lives more closely resembled the life of a recluse. It was as though they were persevering, in a numbed-out sort of way, but not really participating. Obviously these people were getting some benefit from the association, but it didn't look to me to be very much of an experience of community. On the one hand it seems important to honor their choice about how to live their lives, and on the other, it seems a shame to let the weeks and years roll by without offering an outstretched hand of

DOUG JONES

Is there much time and opportunity for just "hanging out"? Getting a haircut at Birdsfoot Farm, New York.

inspiration and encouragement. You never know if the person's choice is a conscious one until you ask, so initiate dialogue … but don't push an agenda.

The bottom line? I don't believe there's one set of practices or beliefs that can guarantee an experience of "community spirit," so the best insurance is to nurture it from many angles. Establish lofty goals, and work together to achieve them. Set up your daily life so you are intentionally and accidentally encountering the other members of your community. Do big and small activities together regularly. Initiate dialogues, share what's important to you, invite reflection and participation. Learn techniques for identifying and moving through misunderstandings and disagreements. Reach out to those who aren't participating much, and appreciate their uniqueness and their gifts. Celebrate what you've accomplished together. And stick with it! It's rare that community happens overnight … but maybe tonight's the night. Ω

Geoph Kozeny has lived in various kinds of communities for 27 years, and has been on the road for 12 years visiting communities: asking about their visions and realities, taking photos, and giving slide shows about the diversity and vitality of the communities movement. His video documentary, "Visions of Utopia: Experiments in Sustainable Culture," will be available in September for $38 postpaid (US), and for FIC members, $33 postpaid. Call 800-462-8240.

Values of the Featured Communities

In my "values glue" matrix, I weighted each of the shared visions/values as follows:

3 = Visions/values of primary importance
2 = Of secondary importance
1 = Occasional, or by individuals
0 = Not currently applicable

I ranked the results from the highest point total to the lowest. The first number is the number of communities out of the 18 that I gave the highest, "3" rating to for that value. The second number, in parentheses, is the total number of points for that value—the "importance" rating multiplied by the number of communities that have that value. In the first instance, for example, I noted that all 18 communities valued "cooperation" of primary importance, hence each got a "3."

18 (54) Cooperation
16 (52) Sense of neighborhood and/or community
14 (49) Equality, democracy
13 (48) Shared resources
11 (47) Safe environment
10 (42) Extended family (shared meals, chores, etc.)
9 (42) Earth stewardship
9 (41) Creating a replicable model
6 (34) Organic farming
6 (33) Children
6 (33) Self-sufficiency
6 (33) Personal growth, interpersonal "process"
5 (33) Being of service in the world
5 (32) Nonconsumerist lifestyle
4 (32) Social/political activism
3 (32) Operating shared businesses
5 (24) Spirituality
5 (23) Conference/retreat/education center

The communities featured in the video: *Spiritual Communities:* Ananda Village, CA; Camphill Special Schools, PA; Catholic Worker House, TX; The Farm, TN. *Rural Egalitarian Communities:* Riverspirit, CA; Sandhill Farm, MO; Twin Oaks, VA. *Urban Communities:* Ganas, NY; Goodenough, WA; Hearthaven, MO; Purple Rose Collective, CA. *Cooperatives:* Breitenbush, OR; Community Alternatives, BC; Fraser Farm, BC; Miccosukee Land Cooperative, FL. *Cohousing Communities:* N-Street Cohousing, CA; Nyland Cohousing, CO. *Ecovillages:* Earthaven, NC.
—*G. K.*

Wisdom from Within, Wisdom from Without

By Karin Iona Sundberg

Soon after moving to Lost Valley Educational Center, an intentional community in Dexter, Oregon, I found one member particularly difficult to resonate with. I did what came naturally—which was to avoid conflict at all costs. I shrank from her sharp edges and worked to soften my own; to see her as beautiful, to understand her perspective, to give her latitude.

One day she said to me, "You know, Karin, I have my part it in too." She asked me to interact with her more, to tell her the truth. She wanted connection and understanding, perhaps to know why people reacted to her as they did. I still felt tentative, but began to offer her my perspective. Though we never became the closest of friends, over time we forged a more trusting bond. I appreciated her strength, and she responded to my warmth. Her willingness to ask for feedback took courage; she created an opening, and light shone in.

We all need each other to see ourselves clearly. In many communities, even those that are spiritually based, we don't always connect from a place of honesty. By honesty I don't mean sharing every judgment. Judgment isn't honest, it's delusion—it's seeing someone else through harsh eyes rather than owning our own discomfort. But to share who we are, what our fears or dreams are, to say the hard thing that makes us feel vulnerable—especially when a lot is at stake—from a caring, responsible place within...can make or break the well-being of family or community. We have to risk. We have to keep our relationships clear.

A community offers a container into which the members can bring specific practices. This works best if everyone is aligned. At Lost Valley, when we brought in new practices meant to connect us more deeply, those who were not aligned left over the next couple years. This was not an easy period, though in retrospect it seems everyone flourished on their respective paths. During the transition, a core group of members held the vision of a connected, enterprising, abundant, healthy community, and over time, we settled into a new rhythm, like spring burgeoning after winter storms.

We learned that having weekly well-being meetings—where we came together to share our personal challenges and triumphs, lessons we were learning about ourselves, and ways we could use support—was vital to having effective business meetings (where we'd make community decisions and manage the conference center).

Without well-being meetings, our business meetings could become bleak and dysfunctional when previously unexpressed emotions clouded issues and made it hard to come to resolution.

LV members and friends dancing around a Maypole on Beltane.

Any topic could incite stubbornness and resistance, and the fear of not being heard would have members pushing for their own private agendas. By keeping communication clear on a personal level, fewer issues became contentious and irresolvable. We were better able to listen to and understand one another.

We held regular Naka-Ima* workshops in which many members of the community participated. Naka-Ima is a practice of honesty and letting go of attachments. One of the founders of Naka-Ima, Jaime Campbell, says, "Nothing can prepare us more fully for a harmonious future than the activity of unraveling the emotional and ideological patterns which make up our own psyches."

We also learned from other practices: consensus process, nonviolent communication, meditation, and we brought in mediators for sticky issues and to help us with overall visioning. In circles we passed a talking stick.

Community Wisdom Lesson 1: Deepen connections with others. In community there is more at stake and more opportunity to come together to resolve challenges. Utilize the potential to learn from one another; emphasize the importance of kind honesty and keeping resentments clear. Experiment with group dynamics.

• • •

Living in community offers an ongoing opportunity to welcome and celebrate the powerful indigenous custom of rhythmic celebrations and rituals. Sobonfu Somé, a wisdom teacher who led rituals at Lost Valley, grew up in West Africa. She has said of her tribe that their life largely consisted of planning for the next ritual, participating in the ritual itself, and talking about the ritual in the glow of the aftermath; then starting again to plan for the next.

"My people the Dagara people live in community. Their life blood is ritual. As a child I never thought much about ritual and its implications. I thought everything was a given and everywhere I went life would be the same as in my little Village." She was asked by the elders of her community to take their teachings to the West. This separation from her roots was shattering. Over time she found her strength, her place, and her power within the radically different culture of the United States by sharing and leading rituals. She says, "My experience being away from my community has taught me that the close relationship I experienced with community was essential for the growth of human Spirit and necessary for peace within the community."

At Lost Valley we sang before meals and when we gathered together each morning before working in the garden. Singing is a simple and powerful way to uplift and literally harmonize the energy of a group. We celebrated the changing seasons by performing rituals on the traditional Celtic holidays and cross holidays (Solstices, Equinoxes, and Imbolc, Beltane, Lammas, and Samhain). On birthdays we exchanged coupons, or promise notes as gifts. Everyone, even the youngest children, would write down (or have helping writing) what they would give—childcare, going for a walk in the woods, a massage, a movie, doing the person's dishes for a week. We had rituals for transitions—initiations into being an elder or a healer, for children letting go of nursing, for becoming godparents, for grieving miscarriage or divorce.

Within the members we had various interests and individual practices, and in addition our conference center hosted groups of different faiths; we were living in the midst of many traditions—Buddhist, pagan, Native American, Jewish, Christian. This gave us all an opportunity to keep expanding our own understanding of others.

Community Wisdom Lesson 2: Deepen connection with spirit. Learn from the wisdom of indigenous cultures; use rhythmic celebrations to infuse the community with a sense of the sacred within everyday life. Have fun together.

• • •

Large Linden trees lined the walk to our office, and I came to anticipate their blossoming each spring. We called them the bee trees, because once the flowers bloomed, you could hear the buzzing from yards away. Watching the bees at work near the lower branches at eye level was a study in wild harmonious industry.

Other perennial rhythms could be counted on as well. Like a well-tuned orchestra, each living thing presented itself with perfect timing, springing from the ground or bursting into bloom...Shasta daisies, morel mushrooms, the rare Lady's Slipper orchids, maple tree blossoms, the slender purple irises that showed up along a tiny seasonal water catchment pond. They all could be reckoned on to rise up in a steady succession, and then recede back to the earth, quiet until their time came again.

Of course in cities we have access to and awareness of the changing seasons. But there was something remarkable about

Author's daughter Grace Kaplowitz communing with nature.

Photos courtesy of Karin Iona Sundberg

living on land year after year, having an expanse of nature outside the front door, walking through the meadow to the office rather than commuting, especially while paying attention, practicing gratitude, and working to improve the environment. Planting gardens, fixing infrastructure, creating sacred spaces, being committed to helping a place and community to flourish—all these gave an irreplaceable sense of being rooted.

One day walking along the drive I came to a deep recognition that Lost Valley was shaping me into who I was—as if I were an extension, or outcome, of this blend of land and community. I marveled at the thought: *I am Karin of Lost Valley*, as if I were springing forth like the growing things around me.

This was not an experience I've had before or since, and yet it feels like a vital missing link in our culture. I'm not sure how to create it, though one aspect seems to be to stay in one place long enough to develop an intimate relationship with our surroundings.

Community Wisdom Lesson 3: Deepen our connection with place; commit to knowing it well. Watch the seasons unfold; tune in to the beauty of nature. Notice how the place where you are (family, work, neighborhood, community) shapes and grows you—that you are "of" a place—and how this elicits an innate responsibility, a sense of stewardship.

• • •

Sometimes an intentional community, or any committed group of individuals, needs support from outside its borders. Nearly a decade of "post-community" experience has given me further perspective on both what worked and where we could have improved by incorporating wisdom from others. Areas of community living that may be challenging, and possible solutions (or at least well-intentioned suggestions), include:

Governance

Consensus is a powerful tool, but perhaps not for every decision a community needs to make. Create a management team that listens to members' considerations and makes decisions on certain issues. Establish a Board of Directors to get support and outside perspectives.

Membership

Accentuate the positive impact of new members and mitigate the challenging aspects. Be clear where (on what physical areas and what types of projects) new members can focus their enthusiasm. Decide when a member has voting rights. There is wisdom in knowing why and how systems were designed before changing them.

Also, consider leaving the long-term vision creation to long-term members. In our community there were times when new members had a huge impact on our direction or commitments, and then left within the year.

Vision

Work to create a clear, succinct, specific vision for the community. The broader the vision is, the harder it is to run a business or create alignment within a group. Having a clearly defined vision can help guide community members in making decisions on directions, opportunities, and incoming people.

Know that even when it's clearly stated, each individual will likely have his or her own interpretation of the vision. In this case, the work of Benjamin Zander, author of *The Art of Possibility*, may be helpful. When we make mistakes or clash with one another, Benjamin advocates that we throw our hands up in the air, smile, and say "How fascinating!" (In the office where I work we have chopsticks with little flags—with the words "How fascinating" on them—that we wave around when we need reminding of these helpful attitudes.)

Struggles and Scarcity Mentality

For unresolved struggles, find a practice or practitioner that can help. There are countless options for mediation, workshops, counseling. Be courageous; be vulnerable.

To resolve lack mentality, bring in trainings for the overall business or individuals if needed—trade retreat time or workshop space for small business coaching for members to create their own businesses. The financial health of each individual impacts the whole. Much free information is available online from small business coaches as well.

Within community and decision-making groups, create study groups to focus on and support abundance. Work on unhelpful subconscious beliefs. Our environment has a big impact on us. If each individual is doing their own work to create an attitude of abundance, this will contribute to the group.

• • •

Those who know me are aware of the challenges I faced in the years I lived at Lost Valley. Being an introvert who loves people, I'm drawn to dive in, and then backpedal like crazy. What abides now in my heart is my deep gratitude for the experience, for the connections that blossomed, for the opportunity to take risks and be held by the strong support of my dear friends and fellow members.

Interacting within community, whether it's a family unit, an organization, or an intentional community, can be rigorous work. Yet I also believe that community is our heritage; that creating community wherever we are is life-giving and essential both for our highest good individually and for our culture. Through community we can create openings—in ourselves, into issues, with nature, beyond the mind—and let light shine in. ❧

Karin Iona Sundberg is a writer, painter, and poet living in Eugene, Oregon. She lived at Lost Valley with her family from 1994-2003, and now makes her living as one of the flock at Hummingbird Wholesale.

---

* Naka-Ima inspired other courses, including Solsara: the practice of opening, which is facilitated by a former member of Lost Valley and held regularly in Eugene and Portland.

Six Ingredients for Forming Communities

(That Help Reduce Conflict Down the Road)

by Diana Leafe Christian

"I found the land!" Jack exclaimed over the phone. As the originator of Skydance Farm, a small forming community in northern Colorado, he had been searching for just the right community land for years, long before he and a circle of acquaintances had begun meeting weekly to create community. He was so sure it was the land, he said, that he'd plunked down $10,000 of his own savings as an option fee to take it off the market long enough for us to decide.

I had joined the group several weeks earlier. I knew nothing about intentional communities at the time. However, it had seemed in their meetings that something was missing.

"What's the purpose of your community?" I had finally asked. "What's your vision for it?" No one could really answer.

That Saturday we all drove out to the land to check it out.

And promptly fell apart. Confronting the reality of buying land, no one wanted to commit. Frankly, there was nothing to commit to. No common purpose or vision, no organizational structure, no budget, no agreements. In fact we hadn't made decisions at all, but had simply talked about how wonderful community life would be. Although Jack tried mightily to persuade us to go in with him on the land, there were no takers, and he barely got his money out before the option deadline.

I became intensely curious about what it would take for a newly forming community to succeed. So over the next seven years, first as publisher of a newsletter about forming communities and then as editor of Communities magazine, I interviewed dozens of people involved in communities forming in the '90s as well as founders of long-established ones. I wanted to know what worked, what didn't work, how not to reinvent the wheel.

I learned that no matter how inspired and visionary the community founders, only about one out of 10 new communities actually seemed to get built. The other 90 percent seemed to go nowhere, occasionally because of lack of money or the right land, but mostly because of . . . conflict.

And usually, conflict accompanied by heartbreak, and often, lawsuits. Many of these community break-ups resulted from what I call "structural conflict"—problems that arose when founders didn't explicitly take care of certain important issues at the outset, creating one or more flaws in their organizational structure. Several weeks, months, or even years later, the group ran into major problems that could have been largely prevented if they had handled these issues early on. Naturally, a great deal of interpersonal conflict arose at the same time, making the initial conflict much worse. I've seen forming communities founder and sink on such issues as:

- *"But our main purpose is not to run a retreat center; that's just a business. We can't spend money on that until we take care of our needs first!"*
- *"What? I have to cough up $10,000 more for 'land development'?"*
- *"My brother can't live here? But he's my brother. I didn't*

Diana Leafe Christian has studied intentional communities since 1992, and edited *Communities* magazine since 1993. She is author of *Forming an Intentional Community: What Works, What Doesn't Work, How Not to Reinvent the Wheel,* and offers introductory and weekend workshops on this topic. She is cofounder of a small community in North Carolina. Email: diana@ic.org.

agree to this!"

- *"What do you mean I can't get my money out again when I leave?!"*
- *"Maybe you think it's important to stay in the room and 'resolve the conflict' but I'm outta here! Have your 'conflict resolution' session without me!"*
- *"Ever since Carl joined we've been dealing with his hurt feelings. It's exhausting. How did we let this happen?"*

You get the picture. While interpersonal conflict is normal and expected, I believe that much of the structural conflict in these communities could have been prevented, or at least greatly reduced, if the founders had paid attention to six "ingredients":

1. Choosing a fair, participatory decision-making process that is appropriate for the group. And if it's consensus, getting trained in it.
2. Identifying their vision and creating a vision statement.
3. Learning what resources, information, skills, and tasks they would need, and then either learning or hiring them.
4. Drawing up clear agreements, in writing.
5. Learning good communication skills, and making clear communication a priority, including ways of reducing conflict.
6. Selecting cofounders and new members for emotional well-being.'

To be fair, a number of well-established North American communities never included many of these structural ingredients at their origin. In the '60s, '70s, or '80s, people usually just bought land and moved on. Some of these communities are with us today, and proud of it.

Nonetheless, I recommend these "ingredients" for communities forming now. Why? Because establishing a new community is not easy. Since the mid '80s through the early '90s, the cost of land and housing has skyrocketed, relative to people's assets and earning power. Zoning regulations and building codes are considerably more restrictive than in earlier decades. And because of the media coverage that highlights any violent or extreme practices of a group, the "cult" stereotype is still in public consciousness, and may affect how potential neighbors feel about your group moving into their neighborhood.

The challenges facing new communities today have convinced me that nowadays community founders must be more organized and purposeful—not to mention better capitalized—than their counterparts of earlier years.

1. Fair, Participatory Decision Making

It's probably pretty obvious that a great deal of conflict would arise if people didn't feel that they had enough say in community decisions, unless the community has explicitly created a structure in which members are not expecting to participate in decisions, such as one where a leader or small group of members make decisions, as is sometimes the case in spiritual communities. So, one of the first things I believe a forming community not structured this way should do is to choose a fair, participatory form of decision making.

Most communities I've observed use consensus. However, herein also lies a source of potential conflict. First, the group needs to know that consensus is right for them, which presumes that everyone has equal access to power. It may not work out if one person is the landowner and the rest tenants, for example.

Second, the group needs to get trained, and, ideally, have a consensus facilitator for meetings. Consensus does not mean, as many mistakenly assume, "We'll just keep talking about a proposal for hours and hours until we all agree." It's far more complex and subtle than that. (See the article that immediately follows, called "Consensus Basics.") Unlike majority-rule voting, in which people argue for or against a proposal and it either passes or not, in consensus the proposal itself is modified as people express their concerns about it. If everyone can support a final revision of the proposal, it passes; if even one person blocks the proposal, it doesn't. Consensus therefore only allows decisions that the whole group can live with and implement without resentment. The process should not take hours and hours. If it does, it means the group is not well-facilitated. A good facilitator schedules breaks, suggests issues be tabled for later discussion, or suggests certain items be sent to committee. Blocking is used rarely, and only when someone, after long and heartfelt soul-searching, feels that the proposal would harm the group in the long run—morally, ethically, financially, legally, or in some other way.

Unfortunately, many well-meaning but untrained groups fall into using what I call "pseudo-consensus":

- *"Everything we decide on must be decided by consensus! It 'betrays' consensus to use any other method."*
- *"Everyone in the group must be involved in every decision, no matter how small."*
- *"We'll stay in this room until we make a decision—no matter how long it takes!"*
- *"I block! This proposal just won't work for me."*

- *"I plan to block the proposal we're going to discuss today. So, since I'm already against it and plan to stop it, there's no need to even bring it up!"*

Consensus is like a chain saw. Consensus can chop a lot of wood; "pseudo-consensus" can chop your leg. While majority-rule voting can trigger conflict because up to 49 percent of the people can be unhappy with a decision, poorly understood and improperly practiced consensus can generate every bit as much conflict.

In the consensus process, deciding on a proposal usually takes more time than with majority rule voting. However, implementing a proposal once it's agreed upon usually takes far less time, since everybody is behind it. Nevertheless, because of the time factor, some community veterans recommend having two, or more, participatory decision-making methods, for example, consensus and one other "agreement-seeking" method, such as 70 percent voting, 80 percent voting, 90 percent voting, consensus-minus-two, or consensus-minus-one, etc. Some cohousing groups have an alternative method in place for when they need to make exceptionally fast decisions, such as when they have a narrow window of opportunity to tie up a parcel of sought-after land, or when they make decisions involving some but not all the members. And some communities may split up the kind of decisions made, for example using consensus for most decisions and an alternate method such as 90 percent voting for decisions affecting property value and only among members with equity in the land.

I learned that no matter how inspired and visionary the community founders, only about one out of 10 new communities actually seemed to get built.

On the other hand, other experienced communitarians caution against using two methods. They assert that consensus is not a method but a philosophy of inclusion, and when people are less able to influence decisions while using a faster method it breaks down the trust and the cohesion of the group.

I believe that the decision-making method best for you depends on whether your group is together primarily to build the physical infrastructure of a community (regardless of what members you may lose due to a faster decision-making process), or for your connection and friendship (regardless of the great land deals you may lose due to a slower, more inclusive process).

Whatever method or methods your forming community chooses, if one of them involves consensus, please get good training in it first!

2. Vision and Vision Statement: "What We Are About"

Your vision is a compelling idea or image that inspires and motivates your members to keep on creating community, to persevere through the rough times, to remember why you're there, and to help guide your decisions. This is not necessarily verbal, but can be a feeling, or an energy presence. It gives voice to your group's deeply held values and intuitions. It is your picture or "feel" of the kind of life you'd like to lead together.

The vision is often described or otherwise implied in your collection of written expressions—your agreements, flyer, brochure, and/or Web site. These documents often include a paragraph or two describing what your community will be like, a list of shared values, a list of goals, often a "how we'll do it" mission statement, and . . . the vision statement.

The vision statement is a condensed version of your vision. The vision statement is a clear, compelling expression of your group's overall purpose and goals. Each of you can identify with it. It helps to unify your effort; it helps focus everyone's energy like a lens. Because it reveals and announces your group's core values, it gives you a reference point to return to in decisions or during confusion or disagreement. It keeps you all inspired, as it is a shorthand reminder of why you're forming community. When times get tough, the vision statement helps awaken your vision as an energetic presence. Ideally it is memorized, and everyone can state it.

The vision statement also communicates your group's core purpose to others and to potential new members quickly: "This is what we're about; this is what we hope to accomplish." It allows you to be specific about what you are—and are not. Some recommend that the vision statement express the "who," the "what," and the "why" of your forming community (and leave the "where," "when," and "how" for the mission statement or strategic plan). I think it's more potent if it's short, about 20Ð40 words.

We have joined together to create a center for renewal, education, and service, dedicated to the positive transformation of our world.

—*Shenoa Retreat and Learning Center, Philo, California*

We are creating a cooperative neighborhood of diverse individuals sharing human resources within an ecologically responsible community setting.

—*Harmony Village Cohousing, Golden, Colorado*

We are a neotribal permaculture village, actively engaged in building sacred community, supporting personal empowerment, and catalyzing cultural transformation. We share a commitment to a vital, diversified spirituality; healthy social relations; sustainable ecological systems; and a low-maintenance/high-satisfaction lifestyle.

—*Earthaven Community,*
Black Mountain, North Carolina

While these vision statements leave plenty of room for interpretation, they are considerably more concrete and grounded than many I've seen. Some newly forming communities represent themselves with flowery, overly vague, or just plain pretentious vision statements, and . . . these are often the first to go bust. It seems that communities with vision statements that are more focused, specific, and grounded are often the ones that actually get built.

It is quite possible that people in a forming group have more than one vision among them—which means that the individuals present may represent more than one potential community. It's crucial to find this out early—before the group buys land together.

Imagine founders of a community with no common vision who buy land, move on, put up a few buildings—and begin to run out of money. Now they must decide how they'll spend their remaining funds. But they can't agree on priorities. Some want to finish the community building because they believe that creating a sense of community is the primary reason they're together, and know that having a community building will help focus their community spirit. Others want to finish the garden and irrigation system because they see their primary purpose as becoming self-reliant homesteaders. Different members have different visions, which they incorrectly assume everyone shares. By this time the members are arguing mightily most of the time, but the core of their problem is structural; it's built into the system. This a "time-bomb" kind of conflict, with members unable to see it's not that "John's being unreasonable" or "Sue's irresponsible," but that each member is operating from a different assumption about why they're there in the first place. So what now? Which members get to stay on the land and which ones must either live with a vision that doesn't fit them or move out?

Identifying a vision and crafting a vision statement is an enormous task, often requiring plenty of discussion, meditation, spiritual guidance, and "sleeping on it," through a series of meetings over many weeks.

Many community veterans believe that consensus is the appropriate process for this critical decision. As Betty Didcoct of TIES consulting says, "the consensus process itself fosters an attitude that can help forge a bond and build trust in your group. When the input of everyone is honored, who knows what might surface—a strong single vision that draws everyone, or multiple visions that suggest the presence of more than one potential forming community."

Other community activists, such as Rob Sandelin of Northwest Intentional Communities Association, suggest not using consensus to determine your vision and vision statement. It's a catch-22: for consensus to work well your group must have a common purpose, and at this point, it doesn't. A group needs a method, he says, (such as 90 percent voting, for example) in which some people can diverge radically from others about what they want in the community without bringing the whole process to a crushing halt. I personally agree with this view, although there are groups out there who employed consensus for the vision statement process and it worked just fine.

It is best if a strong, mutually reinforcing relationship exists between your community's values, goals, and vision and the legal structure or structures with which it will one day own or manage its land and assets. (See the article on legal structures, later in this section.) Identify your forming community's values, goals, and vision early in the formation process, and let these determine your legal structures—not the other way around!

3. Know What You Need to Know

Forming a new community, like simultaneously starting up a new business and beginning a marriage, can be a complex, time-consuming process requiring both business skills and interpersonal communication skills. Founders of successful new communities seem to know this. And those that get mired in severe problems have usually leapt in without a clue. These well-meaning folks didn't know what they didn't know.

This seems particularly true of spiritual communities.

I've often seen founders with spiritual ideals and compelling visions flounder and sink because they had no idea how to conduct a land search or negotiate a bank loan. I've also seen people with plenty of technical or business savvy—folks able to build a nifty composting toilet or craft a solid strategic plan—who didn't know the first thing about how to communicate with people. And I've seen sensitive spiritual folks as well as get-the- job-done types crash and burn the first time they encountered any real conflict.

> . . . communities with vision statements that are more focused, specific, and grounded are often the ones that actually get built.

Consider the story of Sharon, who bought and attempted to develop land for a spiritual community. At first it looked promising. Sharon had received zoning approval for an innovative clustered-housing site plan. She met regularly with a group of friends and supporters to envision and meditate. But over the next 18 months this and a subsequent forming community group fell apart, disappointed and often bitter. Sharon struggled with money issues, land-development issues, interpersonal issues. After two years she said she was no longer attempting community, in fact loathed the idea of community, and didn't even want to hear the "C" word.

What had Sharon not known?

- How much money it would take to complete the land development process before she could legally transfer title to a buyer.
- How much each lot would eventually cost.
- That she shouldn't foster hope in those who could never afford to buy in.
- That she'd need adequate legal documents and financial data to secure private financing.
- That she should make it clear to everyone at the outset that as well as having a vision she was also serving as land developer.
- That she needed to explain that she fully intended to reimburse her land-purchase and development costs and make a profit to compensate her time and entrepreneurial risk.
- That she needed to tell people that, as the developer, she would make all land-development decisions.
- That a process was needed for who was in the group and who wasn't, and for what kinds of decisions the group would make and which Sharon alone would make.
- That consensus was the wrong decision-making option for a group with one landowner and others with no financial risk.
- That they weren't in fact practicing consensus at all, but some vaguely conceived idea of it.

I believe that community founders would experience much less conflict if they understood the need for both "heart" and "head" skills. The latter include drafting clear written agreements; creating budgets, a timeline, a strategic plan; choosing legal structure(s) for land ownership or any planned business or educational activities; learning local zoning or land-use laws; and understanding finance and real estate, site planning, and the land development process (roads, power, water, sewage, etc.).

Not everyone in your forming group needs to have all these skills—that's one reason you're a group! Nor must you possess all this skill and expertise among yourselves. Many successful groups have hired an accountant, lawyer, project manager, meeting facilitator, and so on.

Nowadays community founders must anticipate challenges not faced by communities formed in earlier times. First, "ideal" land isn't ideal if zoning regulations and building codes prevent your developing it the way you want to. Second, if your group wants rural land, a lack of decent-paying local jobs will affect your attractiveness to future members. Difficulty attracting members will affect your ability to recoup early land investment costs, so think about the site relative to available jobs before you buy the land. And third, keep in mind that the initial impression you make on potential neighbors will affect whether or not they will support you in getting a needed zoning variance. If you call your endeavor a community or an intentional community, people may only hear "hippie commie cult." Perhaps call it a center, a project, or even a household, but be cautious with the loaded term "community" until they have a chance to learn, over time, that you're in fact fine, upstanding neighbors.

Forming communities need enough time, money, and "community glue" to pull off a project of this magnitude. To start with, it takes a great deal of committed time and hard work. Even if you meet weekly, you'll often need people on various committees—gathering information, drafting proposals, and so on—in between regular meetings. In my experience, this amount of work is equivalent to one or more group members working part-time or even full time.

It also takes adequate capitalization, often several hundred thousand dollars—for land purchase, land development if needed, new construction or renovation, and myriad lesser costs. As soon as it's feasible, you'll need to know roughly how much money your project will cost. Some people raise the money from others; some fund the whole thing themselves. And please don't put every last cent down on the land. Keep enough available for land development, construction, etc., even if that means buying a more modest parcel.

Elana Kann and Bill Fleming of Neighborhood Design Build, former project managers of Westwood Cohousing in Asheville, North Carolina, recommend that forming community groups understand and accept the difference between what is and what is not in their control. They've observed that probably 95 percent of the major variables involving a forming community are not in a group's control. (Land criteria is in a group's control; land use may not be if local zoning requirements are in place.) The group would ideally have a mechanism for building on each decision and moving forward, rather than meandering or even backtracking, as many groups unfortunately do. They would learn what questions to ask, how to research answers, how to present information to the group, and how to base decisions on the best information available. And, recommend Elana and Bill, they would talk frankly about the required financial and work commitments, as well as other real-world constraints, from the start.

It takes a sense of connection, a shared sense of "us"—the community "glue." This is usually born of group experiences: potluck dinners, preparing meals together, weekend camping trips, solving problems together. Work parties are one of the best ways for people to get to know each other, and not incidentally, great ways to learn each other's approaches to responsibility and accountability. Storytelling evenings are great ways to get to know each other on deeper levels, especially if the topics are self-revealing and personal, such as family attitudes about religion, child raising, or money and social class. Such sharing sessions also reveal issues relevant to community living and shared resources later on.

Gathering this range of skills and information in order to reduce future conflict is complex, time-consuming, and often overwhelming.

Can your forming community afford to do without it? I don't think so.

4. Clear Agreements, in Writing

Many forming communities flounder because they haven't written down their agreements, and when people try to conjure up what they thought they had agreed on months or years before, they remember things differently. Unfortunately even people with the greatest good will can recall a conversation or an agreement in such divergent ways that each may wonder if the other is trying to cheat or abuse or manipulate them! This is one of the greatest stumbling blocks in newly forming communities—and it's so easily prevented.

Many agreements are of course embedded in legal documents such as corporation bylaws, lease agreements, or private contracts. Others are simple agreements with no legal "teeth," but which help the participants stay on track with each other nevertheless. Write out your agreements, read them, and for good measure, sign what you've agreed to, whether or not they're formal legal documents. Keep your agreements in a safe place and refer to them as needed.

What do you need to agree on?

- Who your members are.
- Your qualifications to become a member and the process to do so.
- Whether new people need to attend a minimum number of meetings and be approved by others.
- How new members are brought up to speed.
- How decisions are made, and who gets to make them.
- How meetings are run.
- How records are kept.
- Who takes notes, how are they distributed, and to whom.
- Your group's record of decisions to show new members.
- How tasks are assigned to members, and how people are held accountable for them.
- Expected expenses, how they are to be paid, and what happens in case of cost overruns.
- Any dues structure. (Many groups have found that a nonrefundable investment of some minimal amount such as $100 differentiates those "just looking" from those willing to commit time and energy to the project.)
- Who keeps records of what has been paid.
- Whether such monies are refundable, and from what source.
- Your criteria for whether, and how, people may be asked to leave the group.

Having these and other issues in writing, along with proper legal documents for financial matters such as land purchase, can prevent some of the most heart-rending misunderstandings in the months ahead.

5. Good Communication Skills

Every community experiences conflict—including those which include all the above ingredients at their origin! Interpersonal conflict is a given; it will arise. I believe a community is healthy when it deals openly with conflict and doesn't pretend it isn't there. Healthy communities recognize that community offers living "mirrors" for each other, and an opportunity for faster-than-normal spiritual and emotional growth. Dealing with conflict is an opportunity, not a problem.

Some people are naturally skillful and effective communicators. Most of us, however, probably need to unlearn many of our habitual ways of communicating. Unfortunately, Western culture tends to systematically train people away from any tendencies toward cooperation and empathy. We're taught to be competitive and win at all costs, to see conflict in terms of what's wrong with someone else, and to decide things in terms of "us versus them."

I've usually seen conflicts arise because of a misunderstanding, or when someone wants something he or she is not getting, or wants something to stop, and there's emotional charge on the issue. Conflict is exacerbated when someone refuses to speak up about what they want or need, or asks for it in a way that alienates others. Unfortunately, most people's unskilled ways of communicating about the conflict generates even more conflict than was there in the first place.

Fortunately there are plenty of books, courses, and workshops on communication methods that reduce conflict rather than amplify it.

My personal favorite is Marshall Rosenberg's Nonviolent Communication model. He suggests that most of us respond to something we don't like with an attitude and language that subtly blames, threatens, judges, or criticizes others, even if that's not our intention. His process involves a perceptual shift and a four-step process that defuses the level of conflict. Many other good methods exist as well. (See the "Conflict" issue of Communities magazine, No. 104, Fall 1999.)

Forming communities need enough time, money, and "community glue" to pull off a project of this magnitude.

I believe that the higher the degree of communication skill a forming community has, the greater its chances of success. So I urge your group to develop such skills, including some form of conflict resolution—ideally learned with a trainer. And learn these skills early on, when there's little or no conflict, for the same reason schools practice fire drills when there's no fire. Learning such skills at the outset can help reduce the potential destructiveness of poorly handled interpersonal conflict later on.

6. Select for Emotional Well-Being

Some people believe it's not really "community" unless it's inclusive and open and anyone can join. Others believe a community should have membership criteria and a multi-step process for assessing potential new members.

Some veteran communitarians point out that people will naturally mature in community because of the (hopefully) constructive feedback they'll receive and the natural tendency to learn from the (hopefully) good communication skills modeled by more experienced members. This happens naturally in community; I call it the "rocks in the rock polisher" effect—everyone's rough edges can be worn smoother by contact with everyone else. Many communitarians know people who were really tough to be around when they first arrived, but who were so motivated that they learned fast and became model community members.

My observation of "the successful 10 percent" taught me that it's all in the willingness of the potential new member or cofounder. If he or she has what I call "high woundedness" (hey, don't we all?), it seems to only work if the person simultaneously has "high willingness"—to grow and learn and change. I have seen several forming communities in recent years—even those with powerful vision statements, fine communication skills, and good consensus training—break apart in conflict and sometimes lawsuits because even just one member didn't have enough self-esteem to function well in a group. The person's "stuff came up"—as everyone's does in community—but theirs was too destructive for the community to absorb. When a person is wounded and having a difficult time in life, he or she can certainly benefit from living in community, and, ideally, can heal and grow because of the support and feedback offered by others. But a certain level of woundedness—without "high willingness"—appears to be too deep for many new communities to handle. I believe one deeply wounded person can affect a group far more than 10 healthy people, because of that person's potential destructiveness to the group. Such a person can repeatedly derail the community's agenda and drain its energy.

This seems especially true of a potential new member or cofounder who has been abused as a child and hasn't had much healing before walking into your meeting. The person may unconsciously be desperately seeking community as a safe haven that will finally make things right. Such a person usually feels needy, and tends to interpret other people's refusal to or inability to meet his or her needs as further abuse. The person usually (subconsciously) expects to be victimized, and tends to seek out, provoke, or project onto others annoyance or anger and then conclude, "See, I knew you'd abuse me."

> the higher the degree of communication skill a forming community has, the greater its chances of success.

Where should this person go, besides those communities that are explicitly set up as therapeutic settings? A large, old, and well-established community can often take on difficult and wounded people without damage to itself. A mature oak tree, after all, can handle being hit by a truck. But I don't recommend taking on this challenge if your group is small, or brand new. It's just a sapling, not an oak tree, and still too vulnerable.

How can you determine the level of emotional health and well-being in prospective members and cofounders? One way is through questionnaires and interviews. Let's say you're seeking someone who is fairly financially stable and emotionally secure, who has some experience living cooperatively and a willingness to persevere through the rough spots. Irwin Wolfe Zucker, a psychiatric social worker and former Findhorn member, suggested asking: "How have you supported yourself financially until now? Can you describe some of your long-term relationships? What was your experience in high school or college? If you chose to leave school, why was that? Have you pursued alternative educational or career paths such as internships, apprenticeships, or on-the-job trainings? Where, and for how long? Did you complete them?" ("Admissions Standards for Communities?" Communities magazine, No. 96, Fall 1997.)

You can also ask for references, from former partners, employers, landlords, housemates, and former traveling companions.

I suggest "long engagements"—extended guest visits or provisional memberships of six months to a year, so the group and the prospective member can continue to get to know each other. Sometimes it takes a year to find out what someone is really like when the stress gets high.

"If your community front door is difficult to enter," writes Zucker, "healthy people will strive to get in. If it's wide open, you'll tend to attract unhealthy people, well-versed in resentful silences, subterfuge, manipulation, and guilt trips." Once these people become members, he warns, the energy of the group may be tied up in getting them to leave again.

So the last ingredient is to choose people who've already demonstrated they can get along well with others.

Creating healthy, viable communities is one of the finest projects we can undertake. And we can learn to set systems in place—right from the beginning—that give us the best chance of success.

I know of a new community dedicated to teaching ecological living via a community demonstration model. Its founders mastered consensus and good group process skills and created a new-member outreach process through a newsletter and Web site. They set up telecommuting jobs so they could live anywhere. They conducted a national rural county search, and when they found the right county with no zoning regulations, they took a pro-active approach to finding their ideal land. They raised the necessary land-purchase funds in loans from supporters, and drew up effective agreements, covenants, and nonprofit and lease documents. They set up an impressive internship program to help them build their physical infrastructure. Right now they're living in their new straw bale cabins, eating from their organic garden, and making their own biodiesel fuel. Their new community is thriving. And so can yours.

Legal Structures for Intentional Communities in the United States

by Dave Henson
with Albert Bates, Allen Butcher, and Diana Leafe Christian

Many of us involved in intentional communities have an aversion to legal procedures, government regulation, and taxes. It is often the ugly side of the American fetish for private property, lawsuits, and the corporate form that inspires us to create grassroots democracy and trust-based intentional communities in the first place. However, forming an intentional community where the members seek to collectively own land and buildings, and possibly run a business together, requires that at least some of those involved become fluent in the relevant aspects of property, tax laws, and regulations.

Residents of the United States have inherited a relatively recent tradition of placing the highest value—and legal rights—on private property. The vast majority of cultures around the world for the past many millennia have organized the relationship between themselves and the land they inhabit as community property, or with a sense of stewardship rather than any sense of private property ownership. As we know, the private property model has led to a rule of law that protects private 'rights' to exploit nature for private benefit. Growth is valued above the sustainable management of the 'common wealth' of the natural world. Intentional communities are a return to a more traditional—and more ecologically sustainable—model of social organization. Because we are going against the grain, we will run into all sorts of legal barriers. Persevere! We are reclaiming the traditions of our ancestors, and modeling solutions for our children.

What follows are summaries of the options a group of individuals have for holding land and/or conducting business. While we will primarily be looking at legal forms for owning land, in many cases that same legal form can be used for operating businesses. At times in this article, we will be discussing simultaneously the land owning and business opportunities of a particular legal form.

Options for Community Legal Structures

There are many legal forms that allow an individual or a group of individuals to own real property (land and buildings). Before we examine each organizational form, let's look at some of the more important questions a community should consider while comparing each legal form:

- Does the form fit the values of our community?
- What are the group and individual tax consequences?
- What are the group and individual liability consequences?
- How would the form influence a lender in deciding whether or not to refinance a mortgage or give a loan?
- Does the form set requirements or restrictions for how the organization must divide the organization's profits or losses among the individuals members, partners, or shareholders?
- Do the individual members, partners, or shareholders have to pay taxes on the organization's profits (as well as receiving the tax benefits from losses)? Does the organizational form itself have to pay the taxes, and benefit from losses? Or do both have to pay taxes?
- Does the form allow the group to assign its own criteria for management and economic decision-making

See author biographies at end of article.

authority (e.g., only active members get to vote), or does it mandate specific rules for decision making within a group?

- How easy is the form to set up, and to manage over time? How vulnerable is it to changes in the law, to the Internal Revenue Service (IRS), or to other governmental scrutiny? How much are annual filing fees?
- Does the form limit the group's political activity (as does the 501(c)3 tax-exempt status)? Is that important to our group?
- How easy is it to make changes in the controlling documents of the organizational form, or to manage people's joining with or departing from the community?

For the purposes of this article, I have divided the various methods of holding real property into three basic categories:

I. 'Sole Proprietorship' (ownership by an individual),
II. 'Co-ownership' (ownership by a group of individuals),
III. 'Corporate Ownership' (ownership by an artificial legal entity).

In addition, essentially there is a fourth category, 'Mixed Ownership,' which is where you create a mix of two or more legal forms.

I. Sole Proprietorship—Individual Ownership

Here, an individual alone owns real property and/or a business. That individual enjoys and suffers all the rights, benefits, profits, responsibilities, taxes, and liabilities of such ownership. In a community context, this is one way for an individual community member to operate her/his own business at a community while limiting the impact on the larger community to the terms of any lease agreement she/he might create—say for use of one of the community buildings as a business shop or office.

One form that communities can take is to subdivide a property into individually owned lots and homes, then create an intentional community of neighbors. When the owner dies, the sole proprietorship terminates, and her/his property is passed on by will to her/his heirs.

The relative advantages of typical individual home owning apply, including that this model fits better into the way lenders think about mortgages and refinancing. There will likely be a higher resale value for each home (unencumbered by complex contractual obligations to a larger community). To add more intentionality and legally binding restrictions to the community, the group of individual owners could create a homeowners association (see the 'nonprofit' section of this article). There are only nominal filing and licensing fees for a sole proprietorship.

However, this is certainly the least communal of all options, as the individual or single-family owners are not contractually bound to sharing property, expenses, liabilities, or maintenance and decision-making responsibilities. Further, each individual home owner could sell or lease his/her property without the consent of the community.

II. Co-ownership

This covers a variety of ways a group of people can legally organize to buy and own land and buildings, and to legally conduct for-profit economic activities. Many of these organizational forms differ significantly from state to state, so it is important that you do your own research in addition to the general descriptions you read in this or other books.

1. Joint Tenancy

Joint Tenancy is the joint ownership of a single property by two or more people, where all of the joint tenants have an equal interest and rights in the property.

Joint tenancy can be created several ways: (a) when someone wills or deeds property to more than one person; (b) when more than one person takes title to a property (as when a married couple buys property in California, the deed usually names them as joint tenants); or (c) when joint tenants transfer property to themselves and others (as a way to add more people to your joint tenancy community). All the joint tenants have equal rights to use of the joint property, and all share equally in liabilities and profits. This most often includes sharing all necessary maintenance costs, taxes, and work responsibilities. However, a tenant is solely responsible for the costs of improvements made without the consent of the other tenants.

An advantage of this form is the right of 'survivorship,' which means that a joint tenant cannot will her/his interest in the property, but rather upon that joint tenant's death, the title is automatically passed to the surviving joint tenants. The surviving joint tenants take the estate free from all creditor's claims or debts against the deceased tenant.

The disadvantages of this are significant for most communities, including that a joint tenant may sell or give his/her interest to another person without the approval of the other tenants. Such action causes a severance of the joint tenancy, and the arrangement reverts to Tenancy in Common (see below). Also, if one tenant goes into debt, the creditor seeking collection could force the sale of the property to access the cash value of the debtor tenant's share in the property.

2. Tenancy in Common

Tenancy in common is when two or more people have undivided interest in a property. If not otherwise specified, the presumption is that all the tenants in common share interests in the property equally. The tenants may, however, distribute interest in the ownership of the property at whatever fractions they wish. Taxes and maintenance expenses, profits, and the value of improvements on the property must be distributed in the same proportion as the fractional distribution of their shares of ownership.

A tenant in common may sell, mortgage or give his/her interest in the property as s/he wishes, and the new owner becomes a tenant in common with the other co-tenants. Unlike with joint tenancy, there is no right of survivorship—the property interest of a deceased tenant in common would pass to her/his heirs.

There are not many advantages to use this form for most communities. This is a lowest common denominator legal form, meaning that in lieu of the group creating a more sophisticated and intentional legal form or written agreement, people holding property together are considered tenants in common. The same basic disadvantages as for joint tenancy hold, with the addition that any one tenant in common can force a sale of the property to recover the value of her/his interest in the property.

Intentional communities are a return to a more traditional—and more ecologically sustainable—model of social organization. Because we are going against the grain, we will run into . . . legal barriers.

3. Partnership

A partnership is an association of two or more people who carry on a for-profit business. It is the most common way several people can form a small business together. In the simplest form of a partnership, each partner makes equal contributions, shares equally profits and losses, and has equal share to rights, responsibilities, and liabilities. If that partnership owns property together, a 'tenancy in partnership' exists.

To make the legal side of interstate business easier to negotiate, the Uniform Partnership Act has been adopted in 43 states. It defines a partnership as a for-profit business association where two or more persons are co-owners. The controlling document for a partnership is the 'partnership agreement,' which at a bare minimum needs to state the names and addresses of the partners, the name of the partnership, and be signed by all the partners. It needs to be filed with the county clerk.

Unless otherwise stated in the partnership agreement, every partner can act on behalf of the partnership—including signing contracts and borrowing money—and have that act be binding on the partnership as a whole. This has the potential to be a big problem in that one community member could suffer a lapse of group process and borrow money in the name of the partnership, or buy a boat with the community's partnership checkbook (with the money the community was saving to overhaul the septic system). All the partners are jointly and severally liable, meaning that the whole partnership and each individual partner are responsible for the full value of contracts signed by any one partner. This is typically avoided by putting specific language in the partnership agreement that says something like 'purchases over $100 made on behalf of the partnership must require consensus by the partners at a regular partnership meeting,' or 'no individual partner can borrow money on behalf of the partnership.'

A 'general partnership' is when each partner has all rights of ownership, and each is liable for all the debts and liabilities of the partnership. A 'limited partnership' allows for limited partners to invest, but only be liable for partnership debts and liabilities up to the amount of their share in the partnership. Limited partners have reduced decision-making authority and other rights regarding the partnership. In a limited partnership, at least one partner must be a general partner, and that person or persons are jointly and severally liable for all the partnership debts and liabilities.

There are some advantages to this form. In a partnership, a partner cannot sell or otherwise assign her/his rights in partnership property to another. Similarly, a creditor, wanting to collect a personal debt that an individual partner owes, cannot force a sale or lien on the partnership's property. If a partner dies, his/her rights in the partnership return to the partnership, but the heirs of the deceased partner are entitled to the value of that partner's interest in the partnership. Also, for a community, the partnership form offers maximum decision-making control of the organization—the partners can put into their agreement any decision-making or profit-sharing structure they choose, and, if desired, they can change it over time with minimum legal hassles.

The other major advantage of a partnership is that it has 'pass-through tax status,' meaning that, while the partners are taxed on the profits of the partnership, the partnership itself is not taxed. Similarly, the tax advantages of losses to the partnership are distributed directly to the partners.

However, as noted above, all general partners have unlimited liability, although a strong partnership agreement can help remedy this problem. There is also the disadvantage of the fact that it is cumbersome to add new partners or to have a partner leave. In both cases, the partnership agreement needs to be re-signed by the remaining partners, and filed again with the county clerk. Dissolving a partnership can also be difficult, again depending on the clarity of the partnership agreement. And, a partnership cannot hold accumulated earnings in the partnership, but must pass on the profits and losses each year to the partners.

III. Corporate Ownership

There are several corporate forms that should be considered by a group of individuals who want to hold real property together and/or conduct for-profit or non-profit business as a community.

1. Corporation

A corporation is a legal entity consisting of one or more shareholders, but having existence separate from the shareholders. Over the course of American history, the corporation has been ruled by courts to have the legal status of a 'natural person,' meaning that it has many of the constitutionally protected rights of we flesh-and-blood people, including free speech, rights to standing in federal courts, rights to due process, and extensive private property rights. In the eyes of many, this has led to corporations wielding too much power, to the detriment of the very foundation of our democratic society, and there is a growing anticorporation grassroots movement. That said, let's get back to business of creating alternatives to corporate control of the world: building intentional communities!

The basic corporate form is not the best legal form for a community. Compared to a limited liability company (LLC) or a partnership, the disadvantages outweigh the advantages.

A corporation is a common way to raise capital. It is familiar to investors, and legal precedence has been established for every possible sticky situation. Ownership is transferred easily, and the corporation lives forever: it continues until terminated, surviving the departures and deaths of the shareholders.The main advantage is limited liability. A corporation can often also accumulate earnings over the years and distribute them when the tax advantages are best for the shareholders.

However, profits are taxed twice—once as corporate taxes, then again as shareholder personal income. There is somewhat stringent government oversight, and there are many legal requirements (keeping records, holding meetings, keeping minutes, and filing reports). Incorporation costs, legal fees, and annual registration fees should be considered too.

2. Chapter S Corporation

This form is essentially like a corporation, but with the tax advantages of a partnership or an LLC. In fact, tax filing is based on partnership return.The tax implications of an S corporation are the most complex of any of the similar legal forms—one should consult a tax attorney or accountant about the specifics. I'm not aware of any reason to form an S corporation over an LLC.

An S corporation eliminates the double taxing of the corporation. It keeps the limited liability advantages of the corporation. It allows pass-through of losses to offset income from other sources and is a common way to raise capital. Ownership is transferred easily. Like a regular corporation, this entity continues until terminated, outliving its shareholders of any one time.

However, all profits must be distributed and taxed annually. You can't have over 35 stockholders. And, there are lots of rules—more than a regular corporation. Plus, there are specific limits on who can join as shareholder.

3. Limited Liability Company (LLC)

All 50 states have enacted LLC laws since 1988.There is a move in Congress to make a uniform LLC law so states can have common LLC rules. For many communities who are holding real property and are conducting any kind of for-profit business, this is likely the best legal form to use.

The initial filing fees and annual taxes vary from state to state. An LLC is controlled by an 'operating agreement,' and the participants are called 'members.' The LLC is similar to an S corporation, with its limited liability and pass-through taxation status, but the LLC has substantially fewer restrictions than an S corporation.

An LLC is treated as a partnership for tax purposes instead of as a corporation, if it lacks a majority of the following corporate characteristics: (1) limited liability, (2) continuity of life, (3) centralized management, and (4) free transfer of ownership. The LLC law in most states makes it pretty easy to comply with these restrictions.

> Residents of the United States have inherited a relatively recent tradition of placing the highest value—and legal rights—on private property.

Like a partnership or an S corporation, the LLC avoids double taxation of a corporation. Unlike an S corporation, there is no limit on the number of shareholders. Unlike a partnership, LLC members are not liable for LLC debts. Unlike a corporation, there is no statutory necessity to keep minutes, hold meetings, or make resolutions. The operating agreement can allocate different decision-making rights to different kinds of members (for example, the community could decide that LLC investors are limited to voting only on expenditures which exceed a certain dollar amount, keeping day-to-day decision making in the resident group). Admitting new members is easy, and any type of legal entity can join an LLC, including a person (US citizenship is not required), a partnership, a corporation, another LLC, and trusts. However, an LLC cannot accumulate earnings like a partnership can. It must distribute them the year the earnings are made. Also, annual fees are typically greater than for a corporation.

4. Nonprofit Corporation

Nonprofits are primarily organized to serve some public benefit, and do not provide individual profit. Hence, a nonprofit may obtain IRS and state approval for special tax exemption. Most intentional communities have elected to organize as nonprofit corporations and to apply for tax-exempt status.

As with for-profit corporations, a nonprofit corporation is created by registering with the state—filing a list of corporate officers and articles of incorporation. After receiving state approval, the organization may apply for a federal tax exemption with the IRS.

For those seeking to form tax-exempt corporations, there are many IRS tax exemptions to choose from: cooperative or mutual benefit corporations; 501(c)7 social and recreation clubs; 501(c)3 educational, charitable, or religious corporations; 501(c)2 title holding corporations; 501(d) religious and apostolic corporations; private land trusts; community land trusts; homeowners associations and condominium associations; and housing cooperatives. It is best to decide which category of tax exemption you are seeking before filing articles of incorporation, because the articles may have to conform to certain language that the IRS expects before it will grant a particular exemption. A short section on each of these nine categories follows.

a. Cooperative or Mutual Benefit Corporations

'Co-ops' are often used by consumer cooperatives (such as food-buying co-ops or credit unions), worker cooperatives, or producer cooperatives and are another legal option for communities with good state laws governing cooperative corporations. Co-ops are usually organized as nonprofit corporations; however, some states offer a special 'cooperative corporation' category that is neither nonprofit or for-profit.

In either case, to qualify as a co-op, the articles of incorporation must usually provide for open membership, democratic control (one member, one vote), no political campaigning or endorsing, and no profit motive—that is, a limited return on any invested capital. A co-op also provides limited liability to its members. In some states, members get nontransferable membership shares (instead of shares of stock) with an exemption from federal and state securities regulations. Any members who also serve as employees get tax-deductible fringe benefits.

b. 501(c)7—'Social and Recreation Clubs'

Nonprofit mutual benefit corporations can use the IRS tax exemption 501(c)7, which was created for private recreational or other nonprofit organizations, where none of the net earnings goes to any member. This exemption can be used by a community with land which cannot legally be subdivided, yet whose members are required to put money into the community in order to live there, and who wish to recoup their equity if they leave. Members of a community organized this way 'buy' a membership in a mutual benefit corporation. They can later sell their membership (possibly at a profit) to an incoming member.

The advantages are that, if organized properly, the community would not be subject to state and local subdivision requirements—because members wouldn't own specific plots of land or specific houses. Rather, in a strictly legal sense, they would simply have use rights to any plots or dwellings (although the members' internal arrangements could specify which plots or dwellings each would have preferred rights to use). In addition, members could pay for their membership with a down payment and installments rather than in one lump sum. They would be afforded some liability for the actions of the mutual benefit corporation. They would also have the right to choose who joined the community, which could be an advantage over other land-owning legal entities such as planned unit developments (PUDs) or other subdivisions, wherein the landowners would be subject to federal antidiscrimination regulations if they attempted to choose who bought into their community.

The disadvantages are that 501(c)7 nonprofits can be quite complicated to set up and may require a securities lawyer, as they are regulated by the Securities and Exchange Commission. As such, a 501(c)7 cannot advertise publicly for new members, who are legally 'investors.' Rather, existing members or staff may only approach people they know personally to join them. A 501(c)7 may have no more than 35 investor/members. No donations to such a community are tax-deductible. There are no dividends or depreciation tax write-offs; members are taxed on any profit if and when they sell.

> Nonprofit 501(c)3 corporations must provide educational services to the public, offer charitable services to an indefinite class of people . . . combat negative social conditions, or provide a religious service

c. 501(c)3—Educational, Charitable, or Religious Corporations

Nonprofit 501(c)3 corporations must provide educational services to the public, offer charitable services to an indefinite class of people (rather than to specific individuals), combat negative social conditions, or provide a religious service to its members and/or the public. (The IRS interprets 'religious' very liberally; this can include self-described spiritual beliefs or practices.) 501(c)3 nonprofits may receive tax-deductible donations from corporations or individuals, and grants from government agencies or private foundations. They are eligible for lower bulk mailing rates, some government loans and benefits, and exemption from most forms of property tax. Religious orders that qualify under 501(c)3 may also be exempt from Social Security, unemployment, and withholding taxes in some cases.

In order to qualify for recognition as a 501(c)3, an intentional community must meet two IRS tests. It must be organized, as well as operated, exclusively for one or more of the above tax-exempt purposes. To determine the organizational test, the IRS reviews the nonprofit's articles of incorporation and bylaws. To determine its operational test, the IRS conducts an audit of the nonprofit's activities in its first years of operation.

Many communities have difficulty passing the operational test because of the requirement that no part of the net earnings may benefit any individual (except as compensation for labor or as a bona fide beneficiary of the charitable purpose). If the primary activity of the organization is to operate businesses for the mutual benefit of the members, it fails this operational test.

Even if the community passes the operational test by virtue of other, more charitable, public benefits—running an educational center, providing an ambulance service, or making toys for handicapped children, for instance—it can still be taxed on the profits it makes apart from its strictly charitable activities.

This catch, called unrelated business taxable income, has been a source of disaster and dissolution for some nonprofits because of the associated back taxes and penalties, which can assume massive proportions in just a few years of unreported earnings. Unrelated business taxes prevent tax-exempt nonprofits from unfairly competing with taxable entities, such as for-profit corporations. The IRS determines a nonprofit's unrelated business trade income in two ways: the destination of the income and the source. If a community uses profits from bake sales to build a community fire station (presumably a one-time project related to the community's purpose), the IRS may consider that income 'related' and not tax it.

If, however, the bake sales expand the general operations of the community, or pay the electric bill, the IRS may consider that 'unrelated' income, and tax it.

A 501(c)3 nonprofit may not receive more than 20 percent of the corporate income from passive sources, such as rents or investments. If they are educational in purpose, they may not discriminate on the basis of race and must state that in their organizing documents. 501(c)3 are not allowed to participate in politics—they can't back a political campaign, attempt to influence legislation (other than on issues related to the 501(c)3 category), or publish political 'propaganda.' If they disband, they may not distribute any residual assets to their members; after payment of debts, all remaining assets must pass intact to a tax-exempt beneficiary—such as another 501(c)3.

d. 501(c)2—Title-Holding Corporations

This legal structure is a useful option for owning, controlling, and managing a nonprofit group's property. The 501(c)2 is designed to collect income from property—whether it is a land trust, a retail business, or a passive investment such as space rental. All income is turned over to a nonprofit tax-exempt parent corporation, which is usually a 501(c)3. The tax-exempt parent must exercise some control over the 501(c)2 holding company, such as owning a majority of its voting stock or appointing its directors. The two corporations file a consolidated tax return, which tax software can be helpful with. Unlike a 501(c)3, a 501(c)2 may not actively engage in 'doing business,' except for certain excluded categories such as renting real estate or negotiating investments and a 501(c)2 can receive more than 20 percent of the corporate income from rentals or investments.

Many nonprofit communities, especially community land trusts (see below), find that having both 501(c)3s and 501(c)2s provides a needed structure to both run businesses and manage land and housing. The 501(c)2 limits the community's exposure to conflicts with the IRS over questions of income and possible personal 'inurement,' or illegal benefits.

e. 501(d)—Religious and Apostolic Associations

If a nonprofit community has a spiritual focus and a common treasury, it may apply for this tax-exempt status. (Again, the IRS interprets 'religious' and 'apostolic' very liberally; this can include self-described spiritual beliefs or practices, or secular beliefs that are strongly, 'religiously' held.)

In any case, the 501(d) is like a partnership or chapter S corporation, in that any net profits after expenses are divided among all members pro rata, to be reported on the member's individual tax forms. Unlike the 501(c)3, the 501(d) corporation cannot confer tax deductions for donations.

501(d) nonprofits make no distinction between related and unrelated income. All income from any source is related. However, if a substantial percentage of community income is in wages or salaries from 'outside' work, the 501(d) classification may be denied. A 501(d) can engage in any kind of businesses it chooses, passive or active, religious or secular. The profits are taxed like those of a partnership or S corporation. But, a 501(d) doesn't have the restrictions of a partnership (it doesn't have to reform itself with each change of members), and it isn't limited to 35 shareholders like the chapter S corporations.

501(d) corporations have no restrictions on their political activity—they can lobby, support candidates, and publish political 'propaganda.' They may or may not elect to have a formal vow of poverty. Upon dissolution, the assets of the 501(d) nonprofit may be divided among the members as far as federal law is concerned. However, state law generally requires that any assets remaining after payment of liabilities should be given to another nonprofit corporation.

The substantial advantages of the 501(d) may be outweighed in communities that would prefer to hold property privately.

f. Private Land Trusts

A private land trust is a legal mechanism to protect a piece of land from various kinds of undesirable future uses, like being sold for speculative gain; or to preserve land for various specific purposes—public use as a wilderness area, as rural farmland, or for low-cost housing. A land trust can be set up by an intentional community that has a specific purpose for the land, or simply to preserve it for future generations.

There are three parties to a land trust: the donor(s), who gives the land to the trust for a specific purpose or mission; the board of trustees, who administer the land and protect its mission; and the beneficiaries, who use or otherwise benefit from the land. People or institutions on the board of trustees are selected for their alignment with the goals and mission of the trust and their pledge of support. The trustees represent three separate interest groups: the beneficiaries, people in the wider community, and the land itself. The beneficiaries can be people who visit a wilderness preserve or park, the farmers who farm the land, the owners or residents in low-cost housing on the property, or the members of an intentional community who live and work on the land. The donor, trustees, and beneficiaries can be the same people in a private land trust.

g. Community Land Trusts (CLTs)

A CLT is designed to establish a stronger and broader board of trustees than a private land trust. This is accomplished by creating a board with a majority of trustees that are not land users. Usually only one-third of the trustees can live on the land or benefit directly from it, while two-thirds must live elsewhere and receive no direct benefit from the land. This ensures that any donors or land-resident beneficiaries who are also trustees cannot change their minds about the purpose or mission of the trust, use the land for some other purpose, or sell it. The two-thirds of the board of trustees from the wider community serve to guarantee the mission of the trust since they are theoretically more objective, and will not be tempted by personal monetary gain.

This catch, called unrelated business taxable income, has been a source of disaster and dissolution for some nonprofits because of the associated back taxes and penalties

Private land trusts can be revocable by the original donors; community land trusts are usually not revocable.

Private land trusts and community land trusts are set up as nonprofit corporations, sometimes with a 501(c)3 tax-exempt status. The trust holds actual title to the land, and grants the land residents long-term, renewable leases at reasonable fees.

The original owners of the land and assets cannot get their money out of a community land trust once they have made the donation. Also, once land is placed in a CLT it can be difficult to use the land as collateral for loans.

A CLT is an option for those who wish to ensure that the original purpose for their land and activities continues unchanged into future generations, and are not altered by subsequent requirements for quick cash, loss of commitment, or personality conflicts among the land residents.

h. Homeowners Associations, Condominium Associations

Some communities may choose to organize as a 'planned community'—a real estate term, in which members individually own their own plots of ground and dwellings, and are each members of a nonprofit corporation—a 'homeowners association.' The association, rather than the individual members, owns any community buildings and all the common areas, including land other than the individual plots.

Or a community may organize as a 'condominium,' where the members each individually own the air space within their dwellings, and—as members of a nonprofit corporation, or 'condominium association'—they own an undivided interest in the common elements of the property. The common property includes the structural components of the individual dwellings (roof, walls, floors, foundation), as well as the common areas and community buildings.

Planned communities and condominiums aren't legal structures; they are simply methods of purchasing land. In a planned community, the homeowners association owns everything but the individual units, and it must manage and maintain everything. In a condominium, the condominium association owns nothing, but must manage and maintain everything. Both kinds of associations are often organized as nonprofits, under the Internal Revenue Code (IRC), Section 528.

Under Section 528, such an association is exempt from taxation in acquiring, constructing, managing, and maintaining any property used for mutual benefit. Such tax-exempt 'association property' may even include property owned privately by members, such as a greenhouse, meeting house, or retreat. But to qualify, the private property must affect the overall appearance of the community, the owner must agree to maintain it to community standards, there must be an annual pro rata assessment of all members to maintain it, and it must be used only by association members and not rented out.

The association must also receive at least 60 percent of its gross income from membership dues, fees, or assessments. Also, at least 90 percent of its expenses must be for construction, management, maintenance, and care of association property.

i. Housing Cooperatives

This is a very specific kind of cooperative corporation,

also called a mutual benefit corporation. Housing cooperative nonprofits vary slightly from state to state. In general, however, members own shares in the housing cooperative, which gives them the right to live in a particular dwelling. Although nonprofits don't usually allow shares of stock or stockholders, a housing cooperative does. The number of shares the members buy is based on the current market value of the dwelling in which they intend to live.

The members don't own their individual houses or apartments; the housing cooperative does. The members have simply bought the shares, which gives them the right to occupy the dwelling of their choice. They pay a monthly fee—a prorated share of the housing cooperative's mortgage payment and property taxes, combined with general maintenance costs and repairs. The monthly fee is based on the number of shares each of the members holds, which is equivalent to the dollar value given to the member's individual dwelling.

Personal Versus Community Property

So far we've reviewed ways for a community to hold title to real property. There still remains the question of personal property. Some communities require that, as part of joining the community, some or all of the individual's personal property be transferred to the organization, whether it be a partnership, LLC, corporation, or other form. This might include money and bank accounts, cars, and any other private personal property. Some communities require a 'vow of poverty,' and the giving up of personal property to the organization. Others have certain personal property contribution requirements listed in their partnership agreement, bylaws, or operating agreement. Such agreements can also govern what personal property a departing member or partner may take with them from the organization.

Most typically, the community holds title to the land, and individual community members retain ownership of their personal property. As for the buildings, there are two typical ways many communities work this out.

One way is that a community will hold title to all the homes and shared buildings as community property through its partnership or LLC, for example. The homes and other buildings are then used by community members for as long as they are members of the community, probably for some monthly payment to that partnership or LLC. When someone leaves, there is no need to sell the individual home. This eliminates the problem of having a departing member decide who will take their place in the community, and largely does away with housing cost speculation on the houses in the community. There is most often, however, a need to reconcile that departing member's financial, material, and/or sweat equity in that home. Some communities don't place a value on this at all—when you leave, you leave without equity. Others put simple or complex formulas into their written agreements so that when a person leaves (and it should be expected that it may not always be on the best of terms), there is no question of how to figure what monetary compensation that departing member receives. It is absolutely critical to address this question in your agreements before someone leaves. Otherwise, the irreconcilable differences may force you all into court, to nobody's benefit.

The other way that communities manage the question of who holds title to the buildings, is to have each individual or family own their own home, the improvements on that home, and sometimes the land under and just around the home. The community owns the overall property around which the homes are situated, and manages all of the common lands and common buildings. Often county zoning regulations will not allow for this level of subdivision of ownership, but if it is legal, it lets individuals and families have maximum control over their own homes.

The problem here is when someone wants to leave the community, they have to sell their house. Who decides on the value of the home? This begs the question of who decides whether a community member can build onto their home, thus raising the price of their home if they eventually leave. Does the community set style guidelines? Who decides whether or not to accept a particular willing buyer? These are very difficult questions that need to be addressed in your written agreements.

Resources and Research

As your community meets to craft your legal and organizational structures, focus your discussions on making decisions! It is common to have a two-hour discussion on these topics where real progress and agreements are made, but leave the room without writing the exact decision down. It is impossible to structure the legal organization of your community in one or two meetings, so save the last 15 minutes of each meeting to get down in that special binder exactly what was agreed upon, what the nature of the questions are on the issues where no decision was reached, what was left to discuss, and what the next steps you all will take to continue to move the process along.

My best advice is for you to form a committee of a few people in your community to take on a research project. After doing some work, have the committee present the best options for community legal structures to the whole community for extensive discussion. This may be the one area where your community needs to pay for some legal advice—but do it after your committee has become literate about the questions and options. Ask around for an attorney with experience in tax and real estate law. You want someone who will really understand the 'alternative' nature of your endeavor. A certified public accountant (CPA) can often be very helpful on the tax questions. Remember, an attorney or CPA works for you—their advice on organizational questions is only as good as the community's clarity about what your economic and organizational goals are.

Try the legal clinic at a law school near you. They often offer legal advice inexpensively or for free, and may be able to hook you up with a law student looking for a research project.

The Web is an excellent place to get free legal advice. In doing research for this article, I found many sites with very clear and lengthy legal notes about the options discussed here, such as Rob Sandelin's resource site, at http://www.infoteam.com/nonprofit/nica/resource.html. Search for 'Limited Liability Company,' 'Partnership,' etc., and you will find more than you can read!

Nolo Press, in Berkeley, California, puts out some great self-help legal books, including step-by-step books on how to set-up a corporation, partnership, LLC, or nonprofit. Some come with the papers you need to file on a computer disk. Nolo Press, 950 Parker St, Berkeley CA 94710, USA. Tel: 510-549-1976, http://www.nolo.com/

The Institute for Community Economics (ICE) puts out the Community Land Trust Handbook and other resources on land trusts. ICE, 57 School St, Springfield MA 01105, USA. Tel: 413-746-8660.

Endnotes

1. The entire 'nonprofit' section of this article (part III, section 4) is reprinted with slight revisions from a previous edition of this directory: Bates, Albert, Allen Butcher, and Diana Christian. 'Legal Options for Intentional Communities,' Communities Directory: A Guide to Cooperative Living. Rutledge, MO: Fellowship for Intentional Community, 1995.

Author Biographies

Dave Henson is the Director of the Occidental Arts and Ecology Center (OAEC), a 501(c)3 tax-exempt educational and rural retreat center near the coast in Sonoma County, California, USA. OAEC offers residential workshops and training programs on such topics as organic gardening, permaculture, seed saving, environmental and social justice organizing, landscape and studio painting, and establishing school garden programs. Dave is also a founding member (July 1994) of the Sowing Circle Part-nership and intentional community that holds the title to an 80 acre property, including four acres of organic gardens and orchards and over 25 buildings. OAEC leases from Sowing Circle the use of most of the buildings, gardens and wildlands to operate the learning center. Dave also leads weekend workshops at OAEC called 'Creating and Sustaining Intentional Communities,' and is available for phone or in-person consultation with your community about legal and organizational structures, group process and facilitation, and setting up nonprofit educational centers. For consulting information, or to receive a catalog about the Occidental Arts and Ecology Center, call OAEC at 707-874-1557, write to OAEC, 15290 Coleman Valley Rd, Occidental CA 95465, USA, or visit http://www.oaec.org/

Albert Bates is a former environmental attorney and author of seven books on law, energy and environment, including The Y2K Survival Guide (1999) and Climate in Crisis (1990) with foreword by Albert Gore, Jr. He holds a number of design patents and was inventor of the concentrating photovoltaic arrays and solar-powered automobile displayed at the 1982 World's Fair. He currently serves as President of the Ecovillage Network of the Americas and directs the Ecovillage Training Center, which has helped bring sustainable technology, agriculture, and community to persons in more than 50 nations. He produces 'Eco-villages,' the online journal of sustainable community, at http://dx.gaia.org/

Allen Butcher first got involved with tax law in the early '80s as a board member of the New Destiny Food Cooperative Federation and New Life Farm. He was a board member of the Fellowship for Intentional Community during the period of expansion from regional to continental organizing. He served as Treasurer of the School of Living Community Land Trust. Allen lived at East Wind and Twin Oaks communities for 13 years, becoming a student of comparative economic systems in intentional communities. He has written a series of resource booklets for understanding and developing intentional community. While he was at East Wind, Allen conceived the forerunner of this article for the 1990 Communities Directory. He now lives in Denver, Colorado.

Diana Leafe Christian has studied intentional communities since 1992, and edited Communities magazine since 1993. She is author of Forming an Intentional Community: What Works, What Doesn't Work, How Not to Reinvent the Wheel, and offers introductory and weekend workshops on this topic. She is cofounder of a small community in North Carolina. Email: diana@ic.org.

Buying Your Community Property

by Frances Forster and Byron Sandford

Frances Forster and Byron Sandford offer an upbeat primer on criteria for evaluating property, with special emphasis on the how-tos and how-comes of financing, insurance, and legal considerations.

Buying your community property will be a lot like buying a home. If you've ever done that you know it can be a roller coaster ride, but eventually it does end! The process itself will provide many good opportunities to practice your group decision-making procedures, and test your abilities to trust that your decision to pursue this venture is right.

So where do you start? By answering three simple questions:

(1) Where do you want to be (geographically)?

(2) What do you need?

(3) How much can you afford?

After you've addressed these questions, the next steps are a little more mechanical—after all, there are only so many ways of identifying property and paying for it. Just trust that your decision makers will stay focused on the big picture and not get distracted by the zillion and one (sometimes insignificant) details.

Where Do You Want to Be?

Consider what your members are going to be doing for work and recreation. What are your needs for land, water, transportation, proximity to towns? What are your needs for an audience or market, for schools and continuing education? What about climate, rainfall, or soil types?

Make your lists and consult some maps. Chambers of commerce, local governments, newspapers, and libraries can be good sources of information about places you're considering.

What Do You Need?

A number of things need to fit together, or be developed hand in hand, so you need to have a rough idea of the number and types of people, animals, buildings, cars, and land uses that are going to be a part of the planned picture. For example, your county health department may require a certain type or size of septic system based on the number of people, and the septic fields need to be a certain distance from wells, waterways, and swimming areas.

Operations that require special permits, like the use of chemicals or machinery, merit special consideration, as do services or activities that will bring traffic or require animal management. Check out local ordinances or restrictions related to such spe cial issues now, before you start the property search.

Sketch out a couple of rough site plans showing the desired relationships between buildings or functions. Having these will help in the site-selection process.

How Much Can You Afford?

Unless someone is giving you all the funds (or the land) with no strings attached, you will most likely need

---

Frances Forster and Byron Sandford are part of a new community, Quakerland, west of San Marcos, Texas, to be based on land currently used as a retreat by Quaker meetings in the area. They have traveled to Friends' Meetings throughout the region, building consensus for intentional community use of the retreat land, and recruiting folks to join the Quakerland community. Frances is a licensed real estate broker and Byron, a former mortgage banker, renovates dwellings and apartment buildings for rent or resale.

a loan from a mortgage company, bank, savings and loan, the actual seller, or other lender. This will apply whether you need funds for land alone, improvements (buildings), or both.

The lender will assess your borrowing power based on the collective income, assets, and debts of the persons who will be responsible for the note. These persons will sign the mortgage and deed documents for your community, based on whatever internal agree ment you have. It may be to your advantage to have as many people as possible for cosigners, because it will boost your assets—the lender will like having lots of responsible parties.

To determine where you are financially, gather all your financial records and add up four sets of figures: (1) gross monthly incomes, interest, dividends, child support received, and other predictable income; (2) bank accounts, IRAs, trusts, whole life va lues, stocks, bonds, and other assets; (3) total of all debts (credit cards, loans, child support owed, etc.), and (4) the monthly obligation for these debts.

Once you have your totals, a lender can give you an estimate of how much you can borrow. While the figures will vary from lender to lender, you can get a ballpark estimate of what the lenders are thinking by doubling your cosigners' total annual gross inc ome—this approximates the loan amount; one percent of that amount is your monthly payment. For another approximation, if your cosigners already have a debt load, multiply your cosigners' total monthly gross income by 29 percent—this is your maximum monthly payment (PITI: principal, interest, taxes, and insurance); unless your group already owes monthly debts of more than ten percent of the total monthly income. If your debts are higher, the amount available for the monthly land payments is reduced p roportionately. If you put these calculations on paper you'll see how easy they are to figure.

> After visiting with a few real estate brokers, you'll have to decide whether your group has the time, experience, and contacts to manage the land purchase without professional assistance.

Points of caution about your cosigners: (1) get credit reports for each cosigner early on and take a good hard look at them—you don't want surprises later; and (2) if cosigners are self-employed, make sure the lender considers their income eligible; if you do include future business income in your financial picture, be sure to provide profit and loss statements reflecting past experience.

Visit with Lenders

At this point you have a fairly good idea of where you want to be, what you need, and how much money you have to work with. Now it's time to make introductory visits to senior officers of some lenders in your area. Ask for information on rates, loan alter natives, what other things you need to look at, and if they would consider loaning money to your group (not all lenders make all types of loans). Provide possible lenders with an overview sheet. Remember, you're just gathering information, not making a fo rmal loan application.

Visit with Appraisers and Real Estate Brokers

Make brief visits with some appraisers and brokers who specialize in farm and ranch properties, or commercial or multi-family properties if your community will be in an urban location. Again, your goal is to gather information about the vicinity, the mark et, the possibilities. You should be able to learn about good areas to consider, what the average cost per acre or per square foot is in those areas, and which factors are most significant in determining price in your vicinity. Significant factors include size, location, view, water, type of soil, trees, and proximity to major roads.

Broker Commissions, Inspections, and Appraisals

You may not be responsible for the broker commission—in some places it is customary for the seller to pay the commission to the listing broker, who shares it with the buyer's broker. So payment may not be an issue. Yet, many folks will consider trying to save money by avoiding the use of brokers, or even inspectors and appraisers. On the other hand, professionals can save you money, and a lot of time and energy. Their experience and specialized training can help you to avoid making mistakes. Only if yo u feel you have enough expertise and time should you shepherd a real estate transaction by yourselves.

Another word about brokers. There is some debate in the realty world at this time about whether the buyer's broker will actually represent the buyer or the seller. There's no need to get caught up in that concern if you are honest, fair, shop in the price range you can afford, and don't play games. Then, you'll do fine.

Inspections are usually performed soon after you enter into a contract. The private inspection is a very thorough inspection of structures and systems (electrical, plumbing, heating, and air conditioning, etc.). The inspector is hired and paid by the buye r, and costs in the vicinity of $200. The purpose of the inspection is to acquaint the buyer with the workings of the property and the condition of the dwelling systems.

Appraisals are also sometimes called inspections, but their role is different. Appraisers provide an independent estimate of the dollar value of a property for the lender, usually, or the buyer or seller. The general rule for pricing a property is to lear n what comparable properties (comps) have sold for in the last six months. If the market is rapidly changing, and there are enough comps, the time limit may be shortened to three months, or appropriate adjustments can be factored in for market price changes.

Finding Your Property

After visiting with a few real estate brokers, you'll have to decide whether your group has the time, experience, and contacts to manage the land purchase without professional assistance. If you decide to contract with a broker instead, select one that un derstands your needs, has appropriate expertise, and is willing to put in the time that you'll need, because you'll need plenty of time. Everything about an intentional community buying property is unusual, so you'll need a strong, creative advocate who c an help with the other professionals who are part of the purchase process.

The obvious places to look for properties are the local newspapers and free real estate brochures. Another way of locating property, especially in the country, is to drive around the area you're considering. There may be properties for sale by owners, or listed by licensed agents who are not members of the local board. A broker will also have other resources, which will vary in format from place to place, but will include new listings and properties that are for sale but may not have signs.

For-sale-by-owner is simply that—the owners themselves are handling the sale without the involvement of a listing agent. Sometimes owners have enough expertise to do the job right, sometimes not; they may not realize what is involved other than saving the cost of a commission. Be sure to find out what the picture really is. And if you decide to pursue a transaction with no agents involved, for sure get an appraisal, survey, inspection, and especially title insurance, even if you must pay for it yoursel f. (Please note: For-sale-by-owner is different from owner financing, which is discussed later.)

Properties on the market should have an owner's disclosure statement, or a list showing any problems with appliances and systems, structural items, environmental factors, and any legal issues that may affect the property. These statements are now required in some states for the protection of both the sellers and the buyers. If the property you want doesn't have a disclosure statement, insist on one!

Also check on deed restrictions and zoning regulations for your selected property to make sure you can operate the kind of business you want, or build the kind of buildings you need. Review your rough sketches and needs lists—don't overlook something i mportant!

You've Found the Property, Now What?

Submit an offer. If you've done your homework you know everything you need to know to make a realistic offer. Your offer, generally on standard contract forms, will propose your sales price, method of financing, closing date, and other details. Keep it as simple as possible, and don't ask for insignificant concessions. It's OK to make your price a little below where you want to end up, but you don't want to make it so low you insult the seller. You may be buying a family home, not just some corporate tax shelter. The seller may sign (accept) your offer or make a counter, in which case the house is still on the market. Hopefully you will come to terms quickly and move into the closing period—the evaluation period between contract signing and the closing , or actual property title transfer.

You've Signed, So You're Ready to Move In? Whoa!

Give yourself enough time in the closing period to work up a good case of the jitters—if not this whole process is no fun! Actually, from this point a lot depends on the property and the financing method.

In a nutshell, during the next two weeks you'll do the inspection (if there are any structures), the appraisal, and start the loan process, if you haven't already. The loan is usually the part that takes time—anywhere between two weeks and two months, depending on how much information on how many people the lender wants. After the loan is approved, the boundary survey is ordered and any other contingencies are resolved—which can take a while, too. Then you can close, and that just takes an hour or s o. Then you can move.

While the lender is doing its thing, the title company is researching the property records to make sure, for one thing, that the person selling the property has the right to do so, and that the title will be clear when it is transferred to you. That means that no back taxes, liens, judgments, or other claims will be transferred to you, and that any easements, encroachments, rights of way, mineral rights, or anything else that will affect your usage and enjoyment of the property will be made known to you p rior to closing. Your insurance on the title is forever, so they like to be sure about these things!

The title insurance is usually paid by the seller, with a second document going to the lender. The cost to the seller is usually around one percent of the sales price, and to the lender about $200. A copy to the buyer costs a little less. A copy for yours elves would be a good idea—and if you order it up front the cost is a lot less than if you do it later.

check on deed restrictions and zoning regulations for your selected property to make sure you can operate the kind of business you want, or build the kind of buildings you need. Review your rough sketches and needs lists—don't overlook something i mportant!

Let's Talk Attorneys

Attorneys have a place in the transaction if you want them, and they can be invisible if you prefer. They can prepare and review contracts prior to submittal, during negotiations, and after; they can prepare loan and deed documents; they can order title w ork from a title company; and attorneys can be helpful at closings. If you and the seller prefer to close with the title company, the title company and the lender will simply have their usual attorneys draw up the papers and send them to the title company for closing. Also, in some states, attorneys can still act as brokers. A broker can tell you about local regulations.

Let's Talk Owner Financing

In owner financing, the owner is willing to forego receiving his full equity all at once, and instead will earn interest on his equity from you. Normally the seller will want 25 to 30 percent down payment, and monthly payments at or above market rates, al though he may be flexible on this point. It is very common for rural properties to be financed this way.

Sometimes the owner agrees to carry the note for only a few years until it's a good time (for you or him) to refinance, or sell the note. Don't let the idea that your note might be sold scare you—the note is a commodity, like stocks, that can be bought and sold, but your terms remain the same.

In setting up this note, the seller most likely will want to see your financial documents just as a banker would. The difference is that a private seller may be a little more flexible than regular lenders, which are highly regulated and in most cases must meet required guidelines.

By the same token, you should also ask to see the seller's documents to ascertain either that the note has been paid off, or that the seller has the right to sell the property without paying the note off. If the note has a „due on sale¾ clause, then the o wner cannot sell the property this way, at least not without written authorization from the lender. And that should be reviewed by an attorney.

Also, with owner financing you need to be clear, in your documentation, about who will be responsible for paying the taxes and insurance, and when the title will transfer. Even if you don't use a lawyer or a broker, you should still close with a title com pany to make sure everything is done correctly and recorded with the county clerk. A flawed title can be a long-term cause for insecurity and legal expenses, dragging on for years to a very uncertain outcome.

With owner financing you may be tempted to forego the appraisal, boundaries survey, title search, and title insurance to save money. Think again. And if you decide you can do without one of them, think yet again! Honest mistakes are made every day, and yo ur community's future is at stake.

Aren't you chomping at the bit to get started on this community adventure? Just think of all the things you'll learn, and think of all the opportunities you'll have to practice your group-decision-making skills! It will all be worth it in the end. And you 'll know it!

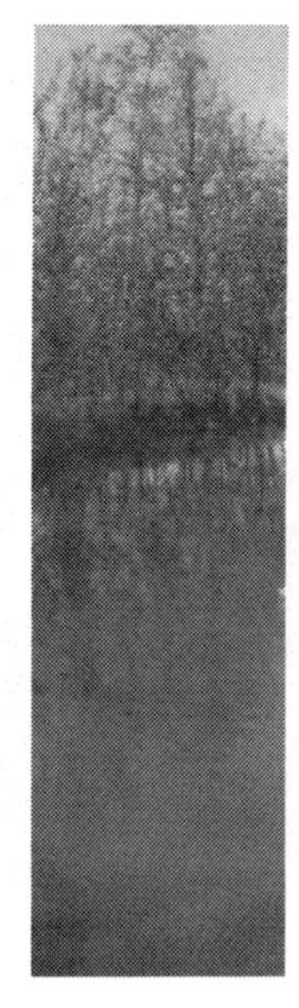

Throwing in the Founder's Towel

By Ma'ikwe Schaub Ludwig

The following article is adapted from a blog entry originally written in mid-2008; because it encapsulates so well the challenges and "hard times" often involved in starting a new community, we reprint it here.

I've just thrown in the towel.

It's not like me, and I'm a bit embarrassed to admit it. But the truth is that I've spent the past seven years working on the rather intimidating goal of starting a residential intentional community, and I've finally admitted that I might not be up to the task. Conventional wisdom says that every new community needs a burning soul, and I've burned brightly, burned joyfully, and finally, burned out.

The first year and a half, I lived with my mother, stepfather, and son, and the three of us adults worked diligently on visioning a community that we could be happy with. But it turned out that our visions were too different, and my relationship with my stepfather deteriorated to the point that it wasn't worth the effort anymore. I had one of my worst-ever human behavior moments about a month before we called it quits, and actually threw a plate during a meeting. (You can't tell me that people can't behave badly and intend well in the same breath!) Garden-variety conflict, combined with a lack of a basic values match, killed the first project.

I spent that next summer at Dancing Rabbit Ecovillage in Missouri. It was a great summer: inspirational, reinvigorating, and just plain fun. But there weren't other kids for my incredibly social son, and I couldn't figure out how to make a living in rural Missouri. I left with some real regret, but the confidence and hope that I, too, could make something like this project happen in the world. So I moved to Albuquerque with a promise from my son's father that we'd start a community together.

The next year and a half was a time of concentrated growth and learning. We rented two houses next to each other in a residential neighborhood, painted the porches a wild turquoise and lavender combination that just screamed "cultural creatives here!," hosted weekly neighborhood dinners until all hours, and supported each other in following our dreams. In a classic example of too-clunky process without much training, it took months to arrive at a name: Sol Space was christened months after we moved in. (Sing it to the tune of "Soul Train," bob your head a little, and you can capture a little of the giddiness when we finally arrived at that one!)

This was the group that supported me in writing a book, having a baby for close friends, and learning about just how important good facilitation is. We shared expenses (and therefore all of our various neuroses around money) and tight quarters (which meant sharing lost its charm fairly quickly and became instead a platform for growth and clarifying what was really important to each of us). Sol Space was a truly amazing social scene...a little wild at times, but characterized by a lot of care and grounding.

Things came apart for two main reasons. The bad news was that we weren't savvy enough about our conflicts, in spite of being creative and dedicated to our friendships with each other. On the good side of the ledger, half of us were chasing bigger dreams: we combined efforts with another cooperative group and began

Photos courtesy of Ma'ikwe Schaub Ludwig

From the left: Welcoming sign to the Dancing Rabbit Ecovillage. Road to the Ecovillage. The old swimming pond is a place of tranquility. The courtyard as you come in: Skyhouse and the Common House. As in traditional villages, courtyards are a big feature for design here, literally holding space for social interaction.

work on a full-fledged ecovillage, wanting to be a model project for urban revitalization. Sol Space was a limited success, short-term but with high impact on a lot of lives, and the initial testing ground for a lot of our ideas and relationships.

So Sol Space morphed into a project that eventually became known as Zialua Ecovillage (or ZEV) and had a much wider draw than the dozen or so folks who lived together in our small co-op. For four years, a typically urban mix of dreamers, teachers, activists, artists, and business people shared a dream of cooperative living. We did our best to correct for past weak points: we committed to consensus training, spent a lot of time working on our vision, and made efforts to get real about money, diversity, and space issues early in the process. It felt, most days, like we were just keeping our heads above the water, but ZEV was powered by inspiration and honesty, and most days that was enough.

I made some huge mistakes as a leader. I confess to pushing the group too fast, being unable to separate my personal needs from the group's agenda, and doing my share of simple whining when things didn't go my way. I also did a lot of things right: got that facilitation training I had been missing, insisted that we learn consensus, connected individually with everyone who showed the slightest interest, and preserved all the friendships I ever made in the process. And yes, I got good at confession, and slightly better at humility.

Things almost fell apart in mid-2006. It was the first period where we started to understand that the three women who had been most central in the leadership of the group had different enough priorities that things were not moving easily ahead. I think, in retrospect, that we loved each other too much and just couldn't bring ourselves to let go of the particular individuals in order to get to the point of having an ecovillage. The wisest of the three of us stepped back into a support role. The other two of us apparently couldn't take a hint: we barreled ahead, convinced we could hold everyone's dreams in one container, if we just tried hard enough.

The wisest of the three of us stepped back into a support role. The other two of us apparently couldn't take a hint: we barreled ahead.

In the fall of 2006, the group landed on a city block with a vibrant, member-owned business, and a development model similar to N-Street Cohousing. This move was an interesting one, and for me, a compromise. We lost people, some of whom were really close friends of mine, and the people who shared the more communal and radical parts of the social vision. I think we lost me, too, though that wasn't immediately clear.

Somehow, I had missed the sweet spot between flexibility and sticking with a vision that inspires me. While the less structured model of community building, in which you let it unfold organically, has huge advantages financially, and also keeps open space for a spontaneity that fed a lot of my companions, it left me feeling flat and unmet in my heart's deeper needs.

I wanted people in my life who were excited to commit to showing up for a shared adventure, not just sharing our tales of the individual ones we were each pursuing. I wanted meals together and a shared vision that we could each contribute to in a meaningful way. I wanted to know that the people I see every day have made a commitment to something bigger than ourselves and that we can lean into each other when we need it. At the bottom of it all, my ecologist's daughter's roots were too strong to ignore, and the chance to really experiment with sustainability outweighed the stubbornness that had kept me at it in New Mexico for five years.

In the fall of 2007, just a year after my group migrated to a city block in Albuquerque, I found myself at the 10-year reunion for Dancing Rabbit. I looked around and realized that the village dream I had found so compelling (and really, had been trying to re-create in the five interim years) was progressing along quite nicely while I was off somewhere

(continued on p. 78)

THROWING IN THE FOUNDER'S TOWEL

(continued from p. 41)

else. And suddenly, being "somewhere else" was untenable. After years of being the "starter," I found myself wanting to join in. And my practical side could finally see it too: enough kids to satisfy even my rambunctious 11-year-old, while the progressed finances of both my life and Dancing Rabbit's suddenly opened a door I had shut, with regrets, five years earlier.

Something else got triggered that weekend, too: in a way I never anticipated, I found myself longing to return to the country. Urban living had worn me thin, and I wanted to wake up to the sound of crickets instead of jet engines, look out at gardens instead of streets.

And so now, almost a year later, I am happily settling back in as the latest resident at Dancing Rabbit, humbled and a bit battered by the lessons and hurts and stretches of the past seven years. I find myself both relieved and inspired to serve a vision that someone else crafted, with a group that happens to hit that sweet spot for me between flexibility and a strong vision. Now when someone wants to know what the hell the founders were thinking, or why we do things like that, people's eyes train on my friend Tony and not me. I feel a little guilty that I am finding it far easier to support him than to be him.

But only a little. I feel like I did my time in that particular hot seat, and am enjoying a well-deserved break and a chance to develop other parts of myself that were put on hold while trying to hold it all together.

What I left in Albuquerque was another qualified success. While the ecovillage never fully manifested, our work over those years spawned a dozen or so meaningful projects that are a legacy of sorts for the Southwest. We still love each other, but now, it isn't "too much" because we aren't trying to make each other fit into a box that doesn't work. The block we claimed is a vibrant neighborhood, in part because we claimed it, and may yet be an exemplary example of what the Fellowship for Intentional Community calls "creating community where you are." In the sense that community means having people who see each other, care about each other, and are genuinely interested in each other's lives, ZEV was (and is) spectacularly successful.

And I've walked away with a profound respect for founders and their unique struggles: feeling responsible for everything, the exhaustion of constantly re-explaining why we are here, and the flashes of joy and pardonable pride when your dream suddenly manifests as a real, meaningful thing (flashes that no one else seems to really grok). Your work has made it possible for me to take the next steps in my own life and, perhaps, finally find my best way to serve and create community. Thank you. ❈

Ma'ikwe Schaub Ludwig lives at Dancing Rabbit Ecovillage in northeastern Missouri, just down the road from Sandhill Farm where her husband, Laird, resides. She teaches workshops on starting communities, consensus-inspired facilitation, and various ecovillage-related topics. She is the author of Passion as Big as a Planet: Evolving Eco-activism in America. *Ma'ikwe is currently involved in something more mundane than starting a new group: building a strawbale house.*

Katherine Pangaro

Sunset over our home in the parking lot.

Emergency Community

By Jesika Feather

Liz McCartney

Aeriel view of the Made With Love Cafe.

Katherine Pangaro

There is still beauty amid the destruction.

Our community fell together in Waveland, Mississippi, post-Katrina. We all found our separate ways to the New Waveland Café, a relief kitchen started by the Rainbow Family days after the Hurricane ravaged the Gulf Coast. When Rainbow gathering meets disaster zone, over-stimulation is an understatement. The hum of the refrigerator trucks eternally cloud the background. Oddly costumed kitchen volunteers stride here and there with boxes of zucchini, chicken legs, mayonnaise, and tomato sauce.

The parking lot where our kitchen was stationed was shared with a distribution center staffed by a church group. Their counters carried everything from evaporated milk and Vienna sausages to fall-themed centerpieces at Thanksgiving. A bird's eye view would show dreadlocks, mini-skirts, and baggy overalls amiably mingled with gray crew cuts and lime green t-shirts reading, "The Church Has Left the Building."

When we arrived in Eugene, we were a crew of traveling volunteers. Now we have a mortgage payment, a baby, full-time jobs, a Subaru wagon, and bags of shorn dreadlocks in the garage.

We washed dishes, chopped cantaloupe, smoked meat, and sanitized surfaces until the city of Waveland could stand on its own, at least as far as pancakes and pulled pork were concerned.

From there we moved on to St. Bernard Parish, Louisiana, where we started a non-profit, Emergency Communities. Our new relief kitchen, The Made with Love Café and Grill, served an average of 1000 meals a day from December 2005 until June 2006.

We came to know one another over the span of months. Our facility housed thousands of volunteers. Each day was a blur of names and faces. Most volunteers were available for short periods of time (one week to one month). Those of us who couldn't bring ourselves to leave, developed a ragtag family.

The parking lot of a destroyed horse betting establishment, Off Track Betting, became our home. A geodesic dome, borrowed from a Burning Man camp, became our dining room. Two long rows of port-a-potties actually started to feel normal. Our pantry consisted of a series of refrigerator and freezer trucks along with a large army tent we named Hot Lips. All this was connected by paths made of pallets—to keep our feet from touching the Katrina-poisoned earth.

For the first time in our lives, cement was clean. Grass was dirty. In the disaster zone, all laws are changed. At least cement can be bleached. It's a quick fix, but it will take years for the earth to heal herself.

None of us are from Louisiana. Like all good hippies, we've eaten our fair share of beans and rice, but apparently we were naïve to the subtle intricacies of Red Beans and Rice, the way "mama" makes it. For one thing, it's supposed to be served on Mondays. The locals pushed their way into the kitchen, determined to teach us about Gumbo, Jambalaya, Bread Pudding, and even fried alligator. We swallowed our pride, handed over our spatulas, and took notes.

Though the action at Made with Love centered around the kitchen, many of my current housemates fell into responsibilities that had little to do with food.

Valisa and Benjah took on the job of reigning in the ruckus that occurs when hundreds of homeless locals, rebellious volunteers, and passionate eccentrics reside in tight quarters. Their work was complicated by the ubiquitous presence of "flood liquor." In essence, Katrina gathered up every liquor bottle in New Orleans and tossed her bounty to the masses. Unopened bottles could be found in trees, streets, and abandoned buildings. Benjah, Valisa, and the other volunteers on security never suffered a boring moment.

Lali, aside from facilitating at least two meals a day, initiated the ritual of "singing the menu." As the residents of St. Bernard Parish waited for the serving line to open, Lali, followed by a convoy of volunteers, wound her way around the dining room. The dancing procession improvised a rhythmic rendition of the menu. The dome echoed with jubilant calls about ham, potato salad, rolls, and peas.

Brian was our rock. As the months wore us down, our already zany idiosyncrasies became increasingly pronounced. Brian stayed solid through it all. He was generally indispensable in every area. Primarily he headed up the First Aid tent but he also washed dishes, provided technical support, worked security and, most importantly, made sure we all wore sunscreen.

I specialized in breakfast. And, because I have an internal alarm clock, I was also the self-appointed wake-up fairy. I crawled from my tent at 5:30 in the morning, still in my pajamas. I pulled on my muck boots and traipsed from tent to tent, rousing volunteers to begin cracking eggs, lighting the griddle, mixing pancake batter, and chopping apples. I picked out a CD—the soundtrack that would define our morning.

By 6 a.m., the kitchen was a hodgepodge of personalities. No one ever had to wake up, but somebody always did. The volunteers were different every day. Sometimes they were hungover, sometimes they hadn't gone to bed yet. Sometimes they were grandmas who effortlessly threw down pancake batter for the masses like it was your average Sunday brunch. Sometimes they were 19-year-old college girls who, when confronted with the prospect of fruit salad for 400, displayed such performance anxiety you'd think they'd never peeled an orange in their lives. Frequently it was gutter punks, conspiring over corned beef hash in a wok—demanding an uncustomary array of spices, swearing "this is how the locals like it!"

Now, when I try to remember us three-and-a-half years ago, it's as if I'm remembering a dream. Those people—pretending they know how to cook green bean casserole with onion crisp-

Valisa Higman

Valisa Higman

Bret Olson

Katherine Pangaro

Valisa Higman

Top left: Benjah takes a moment during the St. Bernard Mardi Gras parade to pose in front of the flood-damaged oil refinery. Top right: Inside Hot Lips. Middle left: Alice and Valisa in front of the domes. Middle right: Hamburgers for dinner at The Made With Love Cafe. Above: Lali, Uncle Van, Heather, Eric, Arjay, Cynthia, Danno, and Kiki enjoy Thanksgiving dinner in the new house. Opposite page: Members of the Heart and Spoon Community after a house meeting. Back row left to right: Evan, Lali, Brian, Valisa, Johnny, Jesika, Lisa, Nathan. Front: Ash and Benjah.

ies, and then serving it to 700 mouths… those people rushing around at 2 a.m., their tents crushed by the weight of the rain, tarping 300 bags of ginger snaps, wondering if the ovens would work in time to cook the frittata. Those people, with filmy June-in-Louisiana skin. Was that really us?

At the end of June, The Made with Love Café and Grill closed down and Emergency Communities founded three new relief kitchens. Our haphazard group of 10 tired, financially pressed disaster relief volunteers crawled into a VW van, a Toyota truck, a Mercedes with no reverse, and pointed ourselves west.

I still can't define what held that tentative caravan intact over the year and a month it took before we sat in an office with a notary and a realtor, signing piles of home ownership papers with a Turkey feather quill.

The year that transpired between starting the ignition on our caravan, and hanging Mardi Gras beads in the window of our new home, was a huge transition for all of us. Whether it was conscious or not, that year led to drastic changes for both our communal and individual identities.

Co-owning a house is a huge financial and social commitment. All decisions affecting our home are made by consensus. This ties us to a considerable financial obligation and a lengthy amount of time invested in communication and conflict resolution with our co-owners.

These choices were not made carelessly. We spent eight months meeting weekly to create the legal document that bound us. During this time, several people realized that this was not a decision they were ready to make. Some backed out entirely, others lowered their level of commitment by choosing to be renters rather than owners. By the time we were ready for signatures, there were five of us still committed to owning.

The eight months we spent creating our legal documents could never be defined as a honeymoon. As far as understanding the personality types we were venturing to work with, we bore no false pretenses. However, there is a certain "reality" surrounding our financial commitment that could only set in over time.

When we arrived in Eugene, we were a crew of traveling volunteers. Now we have a mortgage payment, a baby, full-time jobs, a Subaru wagon, and bags of shorn dreadlocks in the garage. You could say our glamor has been a little…tarnished. Truthfully, if something akin to Katrina struck our country now, we'd be hard pressed to donate our time so freely.

We all have different ways of reconciling with our new identities. I beg someone to play with my son so that I can sit in a coffee shop, eat huevos rancheros, and organize my life into paragraphs. Lali bought a second-hand clothing store and assuages her fears of "normalcy" by wearing and designing the most conspicuously striking outfits in Eugene. Benjah smokes cigarettes with homeless men and swaps theories of impending disaster. Valisa slides recklessly after Frisbees and takes lengthy excursions to other countries. Brian...well, to be honest, I'm not really sure if anything ever fazes Brian. But he, as always, nurtures plants and people.

Our financial commitments have had both positive and negative effects on our community. On one hand, we have a contract that gently nudges us back together when we feel inclined to stray. If there were any glaring issues, we could ultimately end it all, but the added complications keep us from making spontaneous or flighty decisions.

It is imperative that we work through any conflicts that arise. We can't push anything under the rug. We plod our way through agitation about too much dog poop in the yard. We acknowledge fears that some folks get more respect than others, and we hold discussions about whether or not a gun is allowed in the house.

After three years of bi-monthly house meetings and spontaneous breakdowns over sinks full of dishes, confrontation is not nearly the graceless, self-conscious scene it used to be. Now we have a common vocabulary and experiences to draw from. The communication skills we've honed while living together have also pulled us through difficult scenarios in our jobs and personal relationships outside this community.

Our financial commitments have also worked *against* our communal bond. Most of us make the majority of our money by working social services while holding side jobs that involve our other passions. In this way, we manage to serve our larger community while keeping our creative spirits alive. This also means that we work more than 40 hours a week. After prioritizing the nine-to-five job, the art work, the management of art sales, and miscellaneous personal situations, it can be hard to make it home for dinner, much less to attend a house meeting.

Sean Peterson

I know we can maintain this community through a disaster, but I still wonder if we can stick together through the mundane.

It is realistic that after dedicating one year to disaster relief and another year to founding this community, people have to nurture their personal ambitions. If individuals aren't fulfilled, the community cannot thrive.

It is also clear to me that working through intense experiences to achieve common goals is what gave this community its sticking power. Maybe that's why, after we'd signed our names, haggled over rooms, and hefted in the piano, I started to get nervous. What would we do with nothing left to work towards? In my mind, the sweet feeling of success was muted by the fear that we'd reached a dead end. I know we can maintain this community through a disaster, but I still wonder if we can stick together through the mundane.

Within days of signing our homeownership contract, we discovered that I was pregnant. Mostly, I would call this a coincidence. However, I can't deny that with the end of our home-search in sight, I was zealous for a new community project. The idea of a baby, at least temporarily, absolved those fears. As we all know, it takes a village to raise a child...right? Nine months later, reality set in.

Ash, our baby boy, is currently 13 months old, and we are 13 months wiser. My husband and I learned that the ol' "it takes a village" routine doesn't actually apply to the first year of life. Unless the village is so hell-bent on child rearing that they invest in an industrial breast pump and start inducing lactation, the first year

(continued on p. 77)

(continued from p. 27)

Sunset over our home in the parking lot.

is going to belong to the mama. The infant dwells in a very small neighborhood consisting of the left boob and the right boob. He'll broaden his horizons later.

Only in the last few months has Ash begun to belong to our village as a whole. While every member of this household is undoubtedly invested in his upbringing, a community mission statement this child is not. In fact, for my husband and me, he has been another individual project, diverting our attention from the community.

However, when he pushed his five pound, four ounce body into this world, every member of this community was present to cheer him on, and he knew, from his very first breath, that his support system extends far beyond his father and myself.

Now there are days when my life consists of nothing more world-changing than five loads of laundry folded in increments between playing with my son and baking a pie. Each member of our household wakes up to an individual alarm clock, gazes into a day planner blotchy with appointments, and rushes off to nurture the world, individually. I can't help but wonder if we aren't wasting our group potential. While I clean a sink full of eight people's dishes before making myself a bowl of oatmeal, I can't help but wonder…what exactly is the point?

On other days I rush to my job, secure in the knowledge that my son is giggling at home with Valisa. Someone else scours my egg pan, and I glide expertly through quibbles with co-workers. Maybe I am getting something out of this.

I have to remind myself that learning to live together does make the world a better place. That raising my child in a household that faces conflict, but hugs afterwards, is a form of disaster relief. That cooking 10 different dishes, simultaneously, in a very small kitchen, and enjoying it, is a community bonding ritual.

In answer to the question, "what does your community do?" I would have to say, we are growing up together. We are inspiring one another to live to our full potential, and we are squeezing every ounce of passion from the mundane. At least, while I fold the 489th diaper, I can giggle at Lali, in the background, clomping her cowboy boots and singing "Hey, mama rock me."

As I look into the changing faces of my housemates, I remind myself that this is only one of many cycles on our life path. The rich history that binds us is truly a blessing. I should be equally grateful that we've been given this time to focus on our individual needs. Hopefully, in the near future, we'll find a way to combine our service skills to create a new phenomenon of beauty. Let's pray that it won't be prompted by disaster. ❁

For information about current rebuilding projects in New Orleans and St. Bernard Parish: www.stbernardproject.org/v158, lowernine.org.

Jesika Feather is a teacher, mother, and writer. Currently she is a member of the Heart and Spoon community in Eugene, Oregon.

Yes, Wealthy People Want to Live in Community in Sustainable Ways Too!
Fourteen suggestions from those who are trying it

By Jennifer Ladd

In this time of peak oil, climate change, and economic instability, many people are looking to build sustainable community close to home and close to their values. This is true for people across the entire class spectrum, including wealthy people. Money can protect one from many things but we ALL feel the effects of climate change, of extreme inequality, and of the breakdown of people-to-people connection, albeit in different ways. Many people with wealth are looking for ways to leverage their resources for good—to help heal the environment and to support the emergence of a new culture based on cooperation and collaboration. And so wealthy people are playing a role, with others, in the growth of intentional communities and other collective working and living projects.

For over two years, I have been facilitating a telephone support group of people with financial resources who have started, want to start, or already live in intentional community-like situations. The conference calls allow people to learn from one another about ownership models, questions of responsibility and stewardship, vision, clear agreements, and power dynamics. The group alternates between having a support group call amongst themselves one month, then having an outside speaker come to the conference call to share information, experience, or expertise the next month.

Members of this group are located in 10 states from around the US. They come from all different kinds of situations: One person has owned land for 20 years and is now interested in attracting others to live, garden, and work together. One person bought land with the intention of living there with community but the community fell apart. Others bought land or buildings with the expressed intention of turning that property over to community over time either in the form of cohousing, land trusts, or cooperatives. Some group members live in the country, some live in cities. One person grew up on a farm that he expects to inherit, at which point he wants to open it up to others. Some have started out with friends to do this, some have started with a spouse, some have journeyed this road on their own with others coming and going along the way.

The taboo of talking about money and class makes this an important topic. Many of us struggle to have these discussions, but in my 20 years of personal and professional experience working on cross-class projects, I have found it is essential to do so. Whether they are made explicit or not, power dynamics, judgments, and fears exist in this area—along with those related to race, gender, ability, sexual orientation, religion, and so on. The more that each person in a community is committed to examining and understanding their attitudes and beliefs about money and class, the stronger that community, or any community-based endeavor, will be.

The individuals who have participated in this group value building a healthy, sustainable world both environmentally and socially. Each person is looking at their particular circumstances and working to understand how he or she can work with others, and with the resource of property, to embody those values.

But it's not always so easy.

Primary funders can be in control but also feel a great deal of vulnerability as they expose their capacity to fund. Many people have inherited their money. They want to do something of service and they are well aware of how people with a lot of money can be viewed in this time of growing inequality—viewed both with envy/jealousy and with antipathy/resentment. Sometimes they can be seen as an endless source of funding. All told there are distances and differences that need to be acknowledged and grappled with.

Suggestions, Ideas, Considerations

This article is not an exhaustive study of how people with money have started or participated in communities. It is a collection of lessons being learned by this particular sample group—lessons that many others have learned along the way.

1. Encourage early and open discussion of class, money, and power dynamics, realizing everyone plays a part.

Tackle money discussions early on in an open and curious way. Clarify your own values around money, land, and control and ask others to do the same, and then find the structure that embodies those values. Share your class and money stories with each other so you have an understanding of the circumstances and conditions from which you come as you deal with conflict and with moving forward together. Spend time really understanding your own needs and desires for community.

2. If you are someone who already owns property and have a close connection to it, read or re-read the section "When You Already Own Property" (pages 23-24) in Diana Leafe Christian's book *Creating a Life Together.*

She writes clearly about the challenges of forming community when there is one sole owner. She writes, "If you're a property owner seeking to create community on your land…be willing to release total control and find ways for people to become fully participating, responsibility-sharing fellow community members. And if you cannot or don't want to release full control but still want to live in close proximity with others, please do so and enjoy it—but don't advertise it as 'community'!"

Why do some people choose to keep control of the land or property? Well, there are a number of reasons but a primary one is that people have history with the land and care for it. One person has owned her land for many years. She knows its valleys, hills, watersheds, and other resources. She has invested in building a house, barn, greenhouse, and other buildings. She has put a great deal of time and money into a vision and place at which she has much history and many ties. She cares for it deeply. This is also true of another woman who owns land. With others, she has made it a model of sustainability and a place for workshops and retreats. She too has put a lot of money, time, and attention into this land.

Even though both of them feel somewhat burdened by the responsibilities and liabilities and are willing to sell some portion of the land, they feel a great deal of concern for its future care and stewardship and are looking for (and also finding) models of ownership that will assure future care for the land. Members of this group are exploring conservation easements, land trusts, and cooperatives, making the ownership not an individual right/responsibility but a group entity.

3. Be very clear what rights and responsibilities everyone has from the very start.

Most people who own the land/property want to live in community in a way that does not highlight the fact they have the control. They long for a sense of connection and camaraderie. They feel this can't be done if they have the power of ownership and all that it implies. But, in an ironic way, the clearer one is about what control in decision-making the owner has and what others have, the more trust can be established. At least three people in the group have written agreements with renters about their own rights and responsibilities.

4. If you already own property and want to start a community, be as clear as you can about what part of the property you want to hold on to and what part you want the group to own.

One person took the time to determine this, and that clarity has been a relief for all concerned. She says, "One way to share some power, if you are not willing to give it all over to the group, is to have long-term leases for members. Having some more long-term security will allow others to engage more and feel more empowered. Making sure there are plenty of things the group and/or other individuals decide will help a lot too."

5. If you have a very strong and clear vision, do your best to be aware of how the strength of your vision both attracts people and potentially disempowers them from contributing their own vision.

Some people have bought land with a fairly well formed vision of building a program, a school, a model gardening place, a place of retreat and renewal. If the land was bought with the express purpose of achieving a particular vision and mission, it can be difficult to maintain a balance between opening the visioning up to others and keeping the main thread of intent. Sometimes founders are so afraid of betraying their own vision that they become rigid, discouraging other potential community members from fully joining in. There may be ways to let others direct some aspect of that vision for which they have passion and expertise.

6. If you are going to start a community, do so with others, not by yourself.

The danger of finding yourself in an almost parental role is high. You will have to hold all the financial and vision responsibility by yourself to begin with and have to navigate the rocky shoals of transitioning and sharing with others. Yes, have an idea, passion, and vision, but start out as early as possible with others if you can possibly do so.

7. If you do start out with others, get to know and form relationships with those with whom you might build community before living in community together. Take your time.

Allen Hancock, who spoke to the group about his experience with Du•má in Eugene, Oregon, said that if he could do it over again he would have spent more time forging relationships with people in the geographical region where he lives—learn what it is like to work together in some endeavor, get to know people over time—then begin the process of visioning and planning together.

8. If you are starting a community with others, find ways to make living together financially possible AND make sure everyone has some "skin in the game."

It seems to hold true in some people's experience that when community members can come in easily, they often can leave easily. Find ways for people to make proportionately similar financial commitments. One person may have more money than another but the degree of stretch or commitment can feel comparable. Look for structures that will enable others to gain some form of equity or share over time as you, the primary or initial funder, lessens your ownership—cohousing, cooperatives, creative LLC structures, and community land trusts are options.

9. Hank Obermayer of Mariposa Grove in Oakland suggests that there are five skills/elements essential in building community: Visioning, Time and Time Management, Financial Knowledge, Organizational Development, and People Skills.

Make sure that either you or other core members have these assets and as Hank says, "Make sure that the entire core group trusts those skills in each other. Sometimes you need to accept what others in the core group say, without understanding why, when the others have the relevant skill way more than you." Very often (not always) the person with the money will also be the person with more time. Be careful about becoming the default primary mover and shaker because of an abundance of money and time. Look for ways that others can also give meaningful time so that the endeavor is more of a co-creation, while being aware that most others need to work for a living.

10. Consider having shared training in decision-making, communication skills, and conflict resolution.

It can be hard to find the time. Whatever is decided, make sure the group who will undergo the training both chooses to do it and finds some way to help pay for it—again this can be done proportionately so that everyone contributes something. Make sure that this is discussed ahead of time.

11. Building a community takes more time and attention than most people imagine when they start the process.

Be aware of what other activities you are involved in and be ready to give up some things so that you have the time and attention to make living together—and whatever project you choose to work on—successful.

12. Have an exit strategy.

Things can change. Every person in a community most likely will have thought about what they might do if they need or want to leave at some point. If you are the sole proprietor or are the one holding the most responsibility for the land, it helps to think beforehand about how you might leave in a way that doesn't damage the community-like living and working situation. Giving this some thought beforehand may lead you to looking into land trusts or other structures that enable you to follow your life path without disrupting everything that you and others have built along the way.

13. Have a way to get support from others grappling with similar questions, challenges, and possibilities.

I have found that when people are living and working in cross-class situations it is very valuable to have caucus or affinity groups where people can air their feelings and sort out their thinking in order to come back to the group with more clarity and energy to engage.

The people on these conference calls do get support from the people they live with, and it is also very valuable to share ideas with others grappling with similar questions of control, power dynamics, and the confusion of how to live one's values in such an inequitable world.

14. It is absolutely worth it.

Everyone in the group has waded through difficult times living and working with others, but they are also well aware of the pitfalls of isolation, which wealth can bring. People want to be connected with others, want to share, want to find ways to work together with others. All these experiments have helped people to learn about themselves, have provided them with joyful times, have helped people to be better co-creators of sustainable living that we so direly need at this time in history.

As noted earlier, this is not an all-inclusive or even original set of lessons, but they may bear repeating. The more we can openly, collaboratively, and sincerely search for ways of stewarding land and property and living in community in life-affirming ways, the stronger we ***all*** are. ❧

Jennifer Ladd is a philanthropic coach and cofounder of Class Action, a nonprofit organization dedicated to cross-class efforts to educate about and eliminate classism. She lives in Northampton, Massachusetts.

My Advice to Others Planning to Start an Ecovillage

By Lois Arkin

This advice was originally prepared for the book **Eco-Villages and Sustainable Communities: A Report for Gaia Trust** *by the Context Institute (1991), Robert and Diane Gilman. At the point that this was written, I had been engaged in L.A. Eco-Village planning processes for about four years, but had not yet begun LAEV at our current location, nor was there an intentional community when these advisory points were written. Now, after living in an intentional community for almost 20 years, at times with up to 40 persons, here are the original 10 pieces of advice from 1991 and how I refined the advice in 2005 and again in 2011.*

1. **Start with people.** Ultimately, land and buildings are always accessible to a group of people who have a common vision and commitment.
2005 Refinement: A strong vision, good planning, groundedness, and perseverance are the four qualities that will always get you what you need and want, eventually.
2011 Refinement: It takes some of us longer than others.

2. **Develop a core group of people who have some kind of existing track record.** If you don't have one, find those who do and sell them on your vision.
2005 Refinement: Make sure you get a congenial core group of folks with complimentary skills and knowledge who can make a five-year commitment to one another. Then learn to care deeply for one another in relation to the land where you want to work, in relation to the problems with the life support systems in your chosen bioregion, and in relation to the issues in your local political jurisdiction..
2011 Refinement: Learn early how to pick and choose your battles with one another, and do not tolerate unresolved negative conflicts; agree to disagree and love each other anyway.

3. **Don't be in a hurry, but do be persistent and persevering.** We have been very fortunate in focusing on a site that has not been immediately available to us. It's given us the time to develop the culture of the Design Team, develop political and community support, enhance our track record, and attract resources for moving forward. Of course, for a group that already has all that together, this advice is not applicable.
2005 Refinement: It's about process as much as place. So get your team geographically contiguous as quickly as practical, but don't worry about it being your final location. The experience of interactive processes doing ecological, economic, and social work can go with you wherever you ultimately settle.
2011 Refinement: In the world we live in today, it is critical not to be attached to place but to be fully engaged with place where we are. The world-changing work we are engaged in and the pace at which the earth herself is changing may require us to relocate from time to time.

4. **Do not compromise your vision to acquire funding.**
2005 Refinement: Look for creative ways to solve potential funding problems that advance your vision.
2011 Refinement: Often, the less money you have the more creative you are. Our movement is about doing more with less. Brag about it a lot.

5. Keep educating all members of the group on the overview. Provide opportunities for members to learn in informal and exciting ways about all the major systems and sub-systems of an ecovillage: social, economic, ecological.

2005 Refinement: Make the time to do it. Everyone won't have the same understanding, no matter what you do, but they'll bring fresh energy and help the founding core group to see things in new ways too.

2011 Refinement: Institute story-telling as early as possible. You don't have to wait 10 years to share memories. Begin your own rituals as early as possible. Let them flourish.

6. Let your integrity combined with your pragmatism be your guide. Don't be immobilized by ideology.

2005 Refinement: Those who don't agree with the founding vision or have not taken the time to understand it, but enjoy the fruits of the labor of the founders, may try to convince others that you are inflexible, a control freak, attached, stuck in your ways, crazy, evil, and worse. Stay strong, focused, loving, and forgiving in the path of these attacks. But at any point that the shoe really fits, be willing to recognize it, and change your ways. Work on improving your selection process to secure diversity with emotional maturity.

2011 Refinement: Learn to let go when the time is right. What it develops into may be very different than you originally imagined, but you'll have changed too.

7. Don't be attached to the project or being number one. Facilitating widespread sustainability consciousness is the goal; ecovillage is a method of helping people get there.

2005 Refinement: Form coalitions with groups as they come online advocating for, teaching, demonstrating what you have been working on for years. Or once the ecovillage ideas "catch on" in your bioregion, go to the next phase of sustainability, e.g., developing curriculum for local schools, creating your own school, engaging in more public advocacy, writing the zoning codes, giving public talks, civic engagement, running for public office, etc.

2011 Refinement: ...unless you just want to retire to the garden. You've earned it!

8. Do not use or exploit guilt to motivate people, but recognize that many people depend on guilt for their own self-motivation. Help people transcend guilt by keeping focused on the vision. Keep your doors open to fresh and exciting energy. Generate excitement through art, parties, issues-oriented dialogue, etc.

2005 Refinement: Show a lot of appreciation for what others do to generate excitement..

2011 Refinement: Help others to overcome this tendency as well. Learn, teach, use an effective feedback method such as nonviolent communication.

9. Keep borrowing from others; always credit when you can, but if there is not space or time or memory, trust our sustainability networks to know that you are trying to act on behalf of all of us.

2005 Refinement: Recognize others at every opportunity.

2011 Refinement: ...even when they don't really deserve it. Hopefully, they'll be inspired to rise to their publicity.

10. Be gracious, maintain your sense of humor, keep people on track, forgive people from your heart; we're all doing the best we can; keep the air cleared; work at manifesting the values in the processes that you want to live with.

2005 Refinement: Attend to your own health first.

2011 Refinement: Attend to your own health first. ❧

Contact Los Angeles Eco-Village cofounder Lois Arkin at crsp@igc.org; www.laecovillage.org.

Dandelion Village: Building an Ecovillage in Town

By Maggie Sullivan

It may seem impossible to create an intentional community inside an existing city with all the difficulties in zoning restrictions, red tape, and political jockeying. However, Dandelion Village successfully navigated the legal hoops to form an ecovillage within the city of Bloomington, Indiana and their success can be replicated elsewhere. Their keys to success were understanding the process, identifying allies in positions of power, and communicating with complete transparency about their goals and plans.

While rural ecovillages can provide better opportunities for farming and connecting with nature, urban locations have their own benefits, like car-free living, sewer systems, public libraries, better school options, a market for goods produced by the ecovillage, and a more vibrant social scene. Danny Weddle, one of the founders of Dandelion Village, dreamed of creating an ecovillage in his college town and gathered a group of five people who were ready to make it happen. "We looked for a property that was 15 minutes from downtown on a bike," said Danny. Their original vision was of a 50-member community on a permaculture-designed urban farm with members living in small, minimalist cabins and sharing a communal building with the kitchen and bathrooms. This design would allow higher density than typical single family home developments while maintaining much more greenspace and focusing on "hyperlocal food production."

By scouring the property listings and keeping an eye out for "for sale" signs, they located a potential property just south of town. They held a series of work sessions to produce a 14-page ecovillage development plan. At the same time, Danny, Zach Dwiel, and Carolyn Blank set up casual meetings with a few sympathetic city council members, such as the chair for Bloomington's Peak Oil Task Force. These city council members were very supportive and had many suggestions on how to navigate the planning process. Their chief advice was to start talking with the city planning department immediately to determine their options and the best approach for obtaining approval.

Like many fast-growing communities, Bloomington has extensive development guidelines geared towards preserving the exceptional quality of life valued by its citizens. Simultaneously ranked as one of the best college towns, one of the best places to retire, and one of the best gay/lesbian communities, its local culture is artsy, diverse, environmentally conscious, and progressive. Happily, the staff at the planning department was intrigued by Dandelion Village. "Many of the goals of this project...are things the city has been dictating and encouraging through the Growth Policies Plan," said development review manager Pat Shay, commenting on its compact urban form and its use of an otherwise hard-to-develop lot. However, the project was a challenge because it did not meet traditional zoning requirements. "This was a new issue for Bloomington," said planning director Tom Micuda. "We did not have a code for cohousing and that meant we had to go for rezoning for the land. Essentially we did a PUD." PUD (Planned Unit Development) was

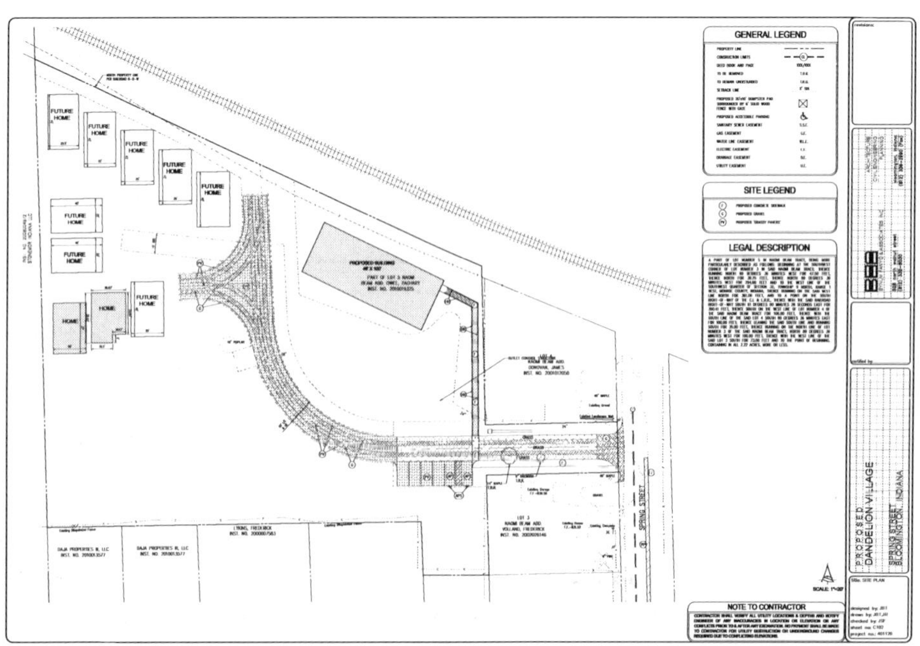

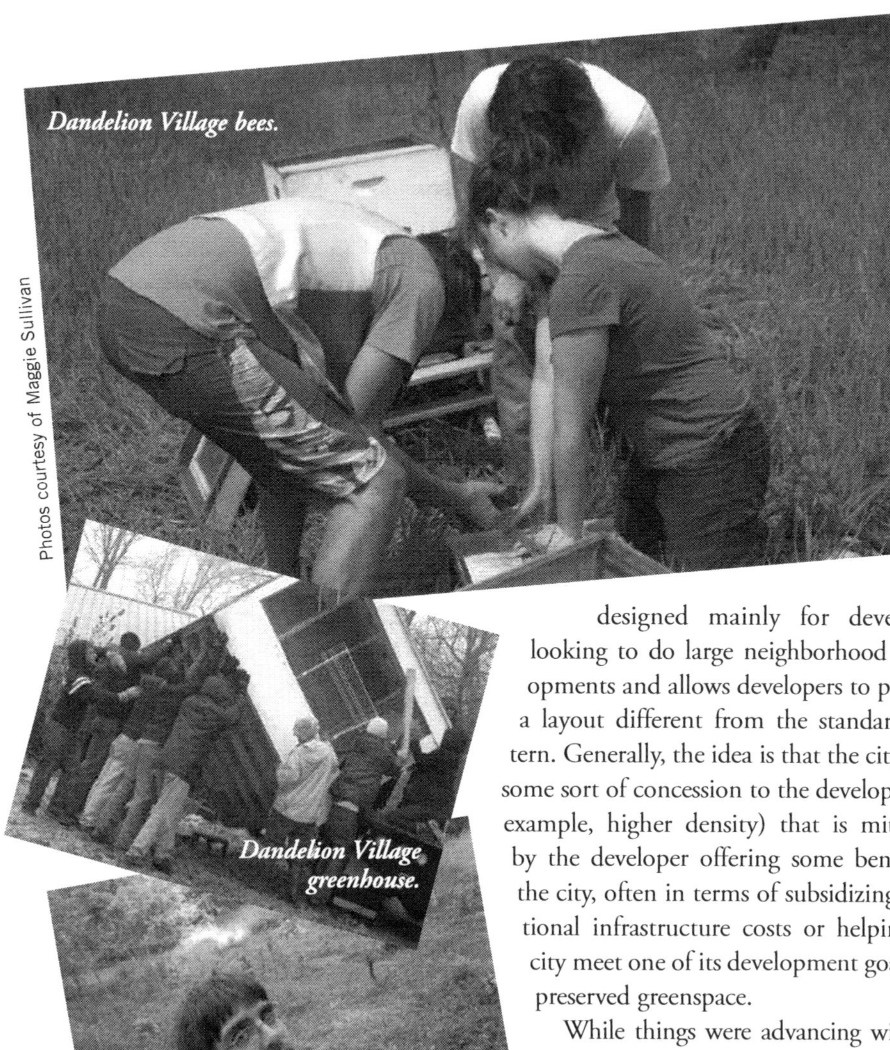

Dandelion Village bees.

Dandelion Village greenhouse.

Daniel Weddle.

designed mainly for developers looking to do large neighborhood developments and allows developers to propose a layout different from the standard pattern. Generally, the idea is that the city gives some sort of concession to the developer (for example, higher density) that is mitigated by the developer offering some benefit to the city, often in terms of subsidizing additional infrastructure costs or helping the city meet one of its development goals like preserved greenspace.

While things were advancing with the planning department, the Dandelion Village group had less success purchasing a piece of land. The owner of the first property raised his price 20 percent, pushing it beyond their budget. Danny, Zach, and Carolyn continued their search via Google Earth and by bicycle. Another promising property fell through before they stumbled on an unusual location that became their ultimate site. It was an odd piece of land sandwiched between a train track, a trailer park, a cemetery, and the blue collar Waterman neighborhood. After conducting environmental studies to determine that there was no contamination from a nearby salvage yard, they purchased the 2.25 acre property for $57,000 and resumed work on the PUD approval process.

Although the Dandelion group had quietly rallied support for months, their first official presentation was to the Bloomington Plan Commission in March 2011. This 11-member board reviews all proposed site developments within city limits and makes a recommendation to the City Council to grant or deny project approval. As part of the process, neighbors were notified of the project and invited to attend the Plan Commission meeting. "In all my years as planning director, Dandelion Village is the most unique project I've ever worked on," said Tom Micuda. "We also had to work through what I would call the fear of the unknown and the fact that ecovillages and cooperative housing are not within the lexicon of standard plan commission members so we had to educate about what that meant."

For the first meeting, Danny and the ecovillage group developed site sketches and proposed development layouts. Their initial strategy was to ask for far more than they thought would be approved, which would allow some room for negotiation. They asked for a density of 15 houses and 75 people as well as site exemptions to allow composting toilets, a large chicken flock of 50 hens, a small herd of goats, barns, and only two parking spaces for the entire development with the understanding that the members would live largely car-free.

Several plan commission members were skeptical of the idea and many were concerned about having farm animals near a residential neighborhood. However, they were impressed by the group's dedication and preparedness and intrigued by the idea of a project countering the "McMansion trend" seen elsewhere in the city. They did advise the Dandelion group that their PUD request would not be approved without plans developed by a licensed engineer. They also listened attentively to the neighborhood residents who came to the meeting and voiced deep concerns. In response, the Dandelion Village group began canvassing door-to-door to talk with their future neighbors and understand their fears.

Most of the concerns revolved around the idea that a hippie commune would bring in drugs and undesirables, not to mention crowing roosters and loose goats eating their peonies. "It was the issue of 'we're not familiar with this—what will it do to us?'" said Tom Micuda. Many neighbors were also concerned about the impact on existing problems like lack of neighborhood parking and flooding issues. The neighborhood streets routinely flooded during large storm events and there were concerns that any sort of development in the area would make it worse.

The Dandelion group continued to talk with neighbors and even helped relaunch the Waterman Neighborhood Association. They also incorporated water retention structures into their site design. Instead of causing additional flooding problems, their development was designed to improve the situation by holding back runoff from the adjacent neighborhood to the north. "We approached from a permaculture prespective," said Danny, describing how they elected to turn waste into a resource. "Water is one of the most critical flows you can possibly have. There has been a drought for the last three years so we said

(continued on p. 77)

DANDELION VILLAGE: BUILDING AN ECOVILLAGE IN TOWN

(continued from p. 48)

'Let's be selfish and hold that water as much as we possibly can.'"

Hiring a watershed engineer was not cheap but allowed them to present a much more professional set of plans to the Plan Commission at their second hearing. Through the negotiation process, they ended up reducing their density to 30 adults and 10 children with 10 small houses and one large communal building that could contain up to 15 bedrooms as well as a large kitchen and dining hall. They had originally hoped that the small houses could be built without kitchens and bathrooms but that would have classified them as a commercial development (e.g. residence camp) and required the installation of sprinkler systems in all buildings—nearly as expensive as putting in kitchens and bathrooms! They did get permission to have both chickens and goats on the site as well as barns for their agricultural equipment. Composting toilets were abandoned in favor of city sewer connections.

The Plan Commission officially approved their request for a PUD in August 2011. By then, public sentiment was generally in favor of the project and the neighbors who had voiced the strongest opposition began admitting some respect for these crazy young people and their vision. Curiosity replaced concern and the project was unanimously approved by the Bloomington City Council in October as an excellent example of walking the sustainability talk.

By this point, Danny and the other ecovillage founders were worn out but happy. They knew there were still three more permitting steps required and they now had the engineering support needed to develop their final plat for the site. In April 2012, they submitted the final plans for review to get their grading permit, which essentially approves their watershed engineering. Simultaneously, they applied for building permits so that the first two homes could be constructed in the summer. As part of their PUD agreement, they must complete all site grading and basic infrastructure (e.g. storm water retention ponds and main roads) before applying for an occupancy permit, which they hope to acquire in the fall. Once the first founders move in, they will start work on two small community houses and the large community building that will provide a gathering space as well as bedrooms that can be rented out to generate income for the ecovillage and house other members as they build their own permanent homes.

The Dandelion group is thrilled by the location and are excited that they have already formed a bond with their new neighbors. "After a year and a half of politics, it feels great to be through the political process and almost ready to break ground," says founder Zach Dwiel. "I'm super excited to start building and stop politicking." While their community has continued to form over potlucks and planning sessions, the members look forward to working side by side building their new home.

Danny acknowledges that this is still the beginning, for both Dandelion Village and for encouraging ecovillage development everywhere. He will be busy for the next couple of years helping the community develop and take ownership of their property. After that, he plans to return to the planning department to propose that their development be used as the model for a new zoning category specifically for ecovillages. "I feel the greatest effect we can have on the ecovillage movement is to set the precedent of a cooperative housing zoning category for the city of Bloomington," says Danny. He hopes this will pave the way for similar developments in Bloomington and even be adopted in other communities. Perhaps someday his ecovillage zoning category will even become the new normal.

Maggie Sullivan is a Bloomington, Indiana native with a passion for sustainability and a deep love of the Midwest. She co-writes the green living blog www.greencouple.com with her husband Will and serves as president of the nonprofit Center for Sustainable Living. Her favorite ecovillage is Lost Valley Educational Center where she studied permaculture in 2005, and she looks forward to having an ecovillage in her own hometown.

Made in the USA
Lexington, KY
18 May 2018